T0328670

Cambridge Elements ≡

Elements in New Religious Movements
Series Editor
Rebecca Moore
San Diego State University
Founding Editor
†James R. Lewis
Wuhan University

HARE KRISHNA IN THE TWENTY-FIRST CENTURY

Angela R. Burt
Australian Catholic University

CAMBRIDGE
UNIVERSITY PRESS

CAMBRIDGE
UNIVERSITY PRESS

Shaftesbury Road, Cambridge CB2 8EA, United Kingdom

One Liberty Plaza, 20th Floor, New York, NY 10006, USA

477 Williamstown Road, Port Melbourne, VIC 3207, Australia

314–321, 3rd Floor, Plot 3, Splendor Forum, Jasola District Centre, New Delhi – 110025, India

103 Penang Road, #05–06/07, Visioncrest Commercial, Singapore 238467

Cambridge University Press is part of Cambridge University Press & Assessment, a department of the University of Cambridge.

We share the University's mission to contribute to society through the pursuit of education, learning and research at the highest international levels of excellence.

www.cambridge.org
Information on this title: www.cambridge.org/9781009065320

DOI: 10.1017/9781009063623

First published 2023

A catalogue record for this publication is available from the British Library.

ISBN 978-1-009-06532-0 Paperback
ISSN 2635-232X (online)
ISSN 2635-2311 (print)

Hare Krishna in the Twenty-First Century

Elements in New Religious Movements

DOI: 10.1017/9781009063623
First published online: July 2023

Angela R. Burt
Australian Catholic University
Author for correspondence: Angela R. Burt, aburt@ochs.org.uk

Abstract: The Hare Krishna movement is a modern manifestation of the Gaudiya Vaishnava tradition, which has its roots in sixteenth-century West Bengal, India. The tradition was institutionalized in a modern form in 1966 when it was registered by A. C. Bhaktivedanta Swami Prabhupada as the International Society for Krishna Consciousness (ISKCON) in New York City. Its mission was to present *bhakti* yoga (the yoga of devotion) to a Western audience. This Element introduces the historical origins of the movement and examines its beliefs and practices within the context of its institutional and community dynamics. It also considers the Hare Krishna movement's changing relationship with mainstream society and its shifting demographic makeup in tandem with key challenges and controversies that have beset the movement throughout its history. The Element concludes by considering how the movement's responses to a new set of issues and challenges are pivotal for its future direction in the twenty-first century.

Keywords: Hare Krishna, ISKCON, new religious movements, Prabhupada, Gaudiya Vaishnavism.

ISBNs: 9781009065320 (PB), 9781009063623 (OC)
ISSNs: 2635-232X (online), 2635-2311 (print)

Contents

1 Introduction and Historical Origins of the Hare Krishna Movement

The Hare Krishna movement has been most easily identified by the sight of young men dressed in orange or white robes and women dressed in colorful saris singing and dancing on the street. The Hare Krishna movement was established when the International Society for Krishna Consciousness (ISKCON) was founded in 1966 in New York City by A. C. Bhaktivedanta Swami Prabhupada (1896–1977), hereafter referred to as Prabhupada (see Figure 1).[1] Prabhupada was an Indian *sannyasi* who arrived in the United States in 1965 for the purpose of spreading "Krishna consciousness" in the West (Satsvarupa das Goswami, 1993c, p. 5).[2] Krishna consciousness refers to meditation on Krishna, the deity of the monotheistic Gaudiya Vaishnava tradition.

Although ISKCON is a modern Western organization, it belongs to a broader and older religious tradition since it is an outgrowth of the Brahma Madhva Gaudiya Sampradaya in the Gaudiya Vaishnava tradition. A *sampradaya* is a religious community, and so the Brahma Madhva Gaudiya Sampradaya is the religious community or the broader religious tradition to which the Hare Krishna movement belongs, and dates back to the sixteenth century. It is within this community that the line of gurus – the *parampara* – passes on the teachings of Gaudiya Vaishnavism to the next generation of students.

Gaudiya Vaishnavism was established in West Bengal, India by the Indian saint Chaitanya in the early sixteenth century. Chaitanya is believed by Gaudiya Vaishnavas to be an incarnation of Krishna. After Chaitanya, the tradition continued by being passed on through a line of teachers (*parampara*) and communities until the late nineteenth century when Bhaktivinoda Thakura (1838–1914), a Bengali civil servant and magistrate, converted to Gaudiya Vaishnavism. Bhaktivinoda introduced innovations in the propagation of Gaudiya Vaishnavism, including the use of the printing press to make Vaishnava scriptures much more widely accessible. He focused his proselytizing efforts on the administrative and intellectual class (*bhadraloka*), which greatly increased the spread of Gaudiya Vaishnavism in West Bengal (Fuller, 2005). His efforts were continued by his son, Bhaktisiddhanta Sarasvati Thakura (1874–1937), who formed a monastic mission called the Gaudiya Math in Bengal in 1920 for the purpose of building on his father's propagation of Krishna consciousness throughout India.

---

[1] Prabhupada means "The feet of the master" (Tamal Krishna Goswami, 2012, p. 22). It is an honorific title his disciples used to address him.

[2] A *sannyasi* is a man who has formally accepted the renounced order of life, or *sannyasa*, which entails renouncing wife and family and paid work in order to focus on spiritual practices.

Prabhupada and the Founding of ISKCON

Prabhupada was born Abhay Charan De in Kolkata in 1896 and was a practitioner of the Gaudiya Vaishnava tradition, taking initiation into the Brahma Madhva Gaudiya Sampradaya from his guru, Bhaktisiddhanta Sarasvati Thakura, in 1932. Bhaktisiddhanta told Abhay Charan that he should spread the teachings of Gaudiya Vaishnavism in the English language (Rochford, 1985, p. 10). This instruction implied spreading the teachings in the West, and had its roots in Chaitanya's vision that Krishna *bhakti* (devotion) would be propagated all over the world (Tamal Krishna Goswami, 2012, p. 33). Abhay Charan followed this instruction by engaging in proselytizing efforts independently due to the splintering of his guru's mission, the Gaudiya Math, over internal leadership disagreements after Bhaktisiddhanta's death (Satsvarupa das Goswami, 1993a, pp. 139–40, 222). In 1959, Abhay Charan entered into the life stage of *sannyasa* in the *varnashram* system.[3] At his *sannyasa* ceremony he was given the name Abhay Charanaravinda Bhaktivedanta Swami and shortened it to A. C. Bhaktivedanta Swami (Satsvarupa das Goswami, 1993a).[4] He would later be given the honorific title "Srila Prabhupada" (Ravindra Svarupa Dasa, 2014), often shortened to "Prabhupada."

In 1965, Prabhupada obtained a free passage to the United States on a ship called the *Jaladuta*. He arrived in September 1965 and traveled to New York City where he gave regular lectures on Krishna consciousness. Prabhupada's classes attracted older, middle-class women and counterculture youth.[5] However, a move to the Lower East Side of New York City meant a new audience consisting mostly of youth who had an interest in spirituality. His following increased slowly but then picked up momentum, and in July 1966 he gave his preaching efforts institutional status by registering an entity called the "International Society for Krishna Consciousness" (ISKCON) (Satsvarupa das Goswami, 1993c).[6] While institutionalizing his new movement through the legal process of registration was in itself an important step, the significance of Prabhupada's charisma in his role as the founder of ISKCON should not be overlooked (Ketola, 2008, pp. 42–3). Prabhupada's ability to attract increasing numbers of followers over the coming years would appear to support this conclusion. In 1967, Prabhupada traveled to San Francisco and established

---

[3] The *varnashram* system is a social system of *varnas* or social classes based on occupation and ashrams or stages of life. The four varnas are: *brahmanas* (priests and teachers); *kshatriyas* (warriors and administrators); *vaishyas* (farmers and merchants); and *shudras* (laborers). The four ashrams are: *brahmacaris* (celibate students); *grihasthas* (married householders); *vanaprastha*s (retired married couples); and *sannyasis* (male renunciates).

[4] Sanskrit is an historical Indo–Aryan language.

[5] The counterculture in this context means, "an alternative culture that differs from the predominant American culture" and refers primarily to "hippiedom" (Judah, 1974, p. 98).

[6] Krishna consciousness refers to constant remembrance of Krishna as the supreme God.

Figure 1 A. C. Bhaktivedanta Swami Prabhupada, New York, 1972. Courtesy Bhaktivedanta Book Trust International. Photo by Bhargava das, used with permission.

a following there, and the movement then spread to other parts of the United States at a rapid rate during the remainder of the 1960s (Satsvarupa das Goswami, 1993b). In 1969, he sent three married couples to the United Kingdom to open a center. The enterprising couples managed to meet with the Beatles and, soon after, they recorded the chanting of the Hare Krishna mantra with the group, which was released by Apple Records and sold 70,000 copies on the first day. Soon after, the devotees appeared on the popular television show "Top of the Pops," singing the Hare Krishna mantra and bolstering awareness of the movement (Satsvarupa das Goswami, 1980a).

In the early 1970s, ISKCON grew at a rapid rate and centers were established in many parts of the United States, the United Kingdom, several other European countries, India, South America, Australia, New Zealand, Africa, and various parts of Asia. Most centers included living quarters where full-time members could live in order to serve the mission. In November 1977, Prabhupada passed away in India at the age of eighty-one. While his death threw the movement into a state of shock, the institution carried on under the leadership of disciples who had already been acting in that capacity for some years; this will be discussed in detail in Section 3.

ISKCON in Context: Hinduism, Gaudiya Vaishnavism, and New Religious Movements

The International Society for Krishna Consciousness is a modern Western institution that is part of the Gaudiya Vaishnava tradition that dates to the sixteenth century. While many scholars of South Asian studies categorize the movement as part of the Hindu tradition, members of ISKCON generally self-identify as "Gaudiya Vaishnavas" or "Vaishnavas," rather than as "Hindu." However, some members of ISKCON also identify as Hindu to align with an established world religion. Similarly, some members of ISKCON reject the "new religious movement" label as inappropriate since the Gaudiya Vaishnava tradition extends back to the sixteenth century.[7] Knott (personal communication, 2006) argues that although the broader Vaishnava tradition of which ISKCON is a part dates back thousands of years, ISKCON as an institution is new, founded only in 1966. Melton makes this point in a more nuanced fashion, arguing that recognizing the roots of new religions contextualizes them within the movement of world religions to the West, and understanding the modern diffusion of the world's religions helps us understand the seemingly sudden emergence of "new" religions in a Western context (Melton, 2007a, p. 31).

To add another layer of nuance to an already fraught exercise in categorization, Haddon (2013b) argues that the attempt to categorize ISKCON is further complicated by the fact that there has been continual cross-cultural traffic between India and the United States as well as other Western countries since the movement's inception in the West. For this reason, the transnational Hare Krishna movement today cannot be understood entirely with reference to a Western sociological frame (see also Burt, 2013), or essentialist, ahistorical notions of Indian tradition. Haddon proposes a more sophisticated understanding of ISKCON's cross-cultural development.

Introvigne (1997) argues that the use of the new religious movement label is better than the label of "cult," which can be used as tool of discrimination. Nevertheless, the former can still lead to misunderstandings about movements

---

[7] See, for example, Mukunda Goswami (1995).

such as ISKCON, which are new only in the West and represent much older traditions in their countries of origin. The most neutral term in his opinion is "religious minorities" because it avoids judgments about whether a group is acceptable or connected to an old tradition. Vande Berg and Kniss (2008, p. 100) suggest that new religious movements are often not all that new; rather, they may combine and adapt previous religious forms to create something that becomes innovative and new.

Therefore, while the label "new religious movement" is an easy categorization, the presence of "new" in that label may gloss over the fact that a modern organization like ISKCON is a development of a much older tradition. Such a tendency can prevent a deeper understanding of a tradition and its rich history. This author takes the stance that while ISKCON can be categorized as a new religious movement, since it was founded in 1966, this movement is part of a religious tradition that dates back to the sixteenth century. Many new religious movements take a syncretic approach, borrowing aspects of various religious traditions and merging them into a new form. However, ISKCON represents a movement that has essentially imported a religious tradition in its totality, with adaptations for a modern Western following. A key theme running throughout this Element is the idea that the Hare Krishna movement can be simultaneously thought of as the continuation of a 500-year-old religious tradition and a new religious movement (Melton, 1987, 2004, 2007a, 2007b), although, as the movement ages, the label becomes less applicable.

While the Hare Krishna movement is a rubric for an array of groups, on an institutional level the largest of these organizations is ISKCON. Until the death of ISKCON's founder in 1977, the Hare Krishna movement and ISKCON could be considered one and the same. However, ISKCON faced factionalism and schism in the late 1970s, resulting in the emergence of several social movement organizations within the broader Hare Krishna movement (Rochford, 1989, p. 163). Since the lines between these different groups are sometimes sharply drawn and sometimes not, it is not always possible to make neat distinctions between them, and between members, former members, and apostates, for reasons that will be discussed in Section 3. In addition, ISKCON as an institution is more than the institutional structure of its corporate form. The historical fact of ISKCON as key to the genesis of the Hare Krishna movement cannot be ignored. As ISKCON is often thought of as synonymous with the Hare Krishna movement, ISKCON devotees are known as Hare Krishnas, both internally and by the wider public. Consequently, the two terms are sometimes used interchangeably and sometimes a distinction is made between them. For these reasons, this Element will embrace both terms as part of acknowledging the history and the lived experience of current and former members, while noting the context-dependent differences that exist between them.

Previous Scholarly Work on the Hare Krishna Movement

A number of monographs published in the 1970s and 1980s provided scholarly analyses of the Hare Krishna movement that considered the prevailing social and cultural contexts shaping the movement's expansion in the West. The most recent monograph that looked at the movement as a whole was published by E. Burke Rochford (2007a). Two edited volumes comprising interviews with academics were published by Dwyer and Cole, the last in 2013 (Dwyer and Cole, 2007, 2013). Monographs from the early 2000s are focused on particular aspects of the movement. For example, Fahy (2019) takes a look at the community in Mayapura, and Karapanagiotis (2021) focuses her analyses on the evolving outreach programs within the movement. Therefore, a monograph is needed that addresses the multitude of issues facing the movement, that takes into account major social and cultural upheavals that have taken place since the scholarly analyses of the early 2000s, and that draws on recent scholarship. This Element aims to fill that gap.

It is important to acknowledge that much of the scholarly work on the Hare Krishna movement to date is based on fieldwork in the United States in the 1970s, 1980s, and 1990s. Most noteworthy among this scholarship are works by Judah (1974); Daner (1976); Rochford (1982, 1985, 1988, 1989, 1998, 1999); and Rochford and Heinlein (1998). Knott (1986, 1993, 1994, 1995a, 1995b, 1995c, 2004) carried out her fieldwork in the United Kingdom, and Hopkins, whose early work was based in the United States, reflected upon the movement as a whole in his later work (Hopkins, 1989, 1998, 1999). More recent scholarship based on fieldwork in the United States in the early 2000s includes Rochford (2007a, 2007b, 2009, 2016, 2018, 2020); Vande Berg and Kniss (2008); Lucia (2015); and Karapanagiotis (2021). This focus on the American experience is justified to some degree since the movement was founded in the United States and from there spread globally with an American influence. However, it needs to be borne in mind that the conclusions from this research do not entirely represent what is going on in the movement globally or in other Western countries. For this reason, the Element will draw on recent scholarship that is based on research conducted in other parts of the world in an attempt to provide a more nuanced understanding of the movement.

My encounters with ISKCON communities have indicated that Rochford's findings, for example, are generalizable to some extent.[8] Regional differences

---

[8] Rochford's work is noted here because he is by far the most prolific scholar of the Hare Krishna movement.

where the Indian cultural influence is greater than the Western influence can be seen, for example, in Fiji, which has a large Indian and Hindu population. In fact, ISKCON membership is almost 100 percent Indian in Fiji. The same may be the case for other countries where local and Indian cultures have more influence. This, of course, indicates the need to increase research in locations outside of the United States, including Europe and Australasia, but also to extend it to areas neglected by research, including Russia, Ukraine, Africa, the Middle East, Asia, and South America. Fortunately, there has been a variety of research since the beginning of the twenty-first century based on fieldwork addressing different aspects of the movement in the United States, Europe, India, South America, Australia, and the Middle East. This Element aims to bring this scholarship together in one volume for a twenty-first-century audience. Of note is anthropological fieldwork in Australian Hare Krishna communities by Haddon (2013a, 2013b, 2013c) and an ethnographic study of the ISKCON temple community in Mumbai by Robison (2016). Anthropological fieldwork has been conducted in ISKCON's flagship temple community in Mayapura, India by Fahy (2017, 2018, 2019b, 2019a) and Mitsuhara (2019). Čargonja (2022) has studied Hare Krishna devotees' religious experience of a personal relationship with Krishna by conducting research at communities in Croatia, Germany, Belgium, the United Kingdom, and India (Vrindavan, Mayapura, and Jagannath Puri).

My own fieldwork consisting of interviews for the ISKCON Oral History Project in the United States, the United Kingdom, Canada, India, Australia, New Zealand, and Fiji has involved interviewing members from across the globe. American devotees are highly represented in this cohort – largely because the movement started in the United States. My research has focused on the early members in order to capture the history of the movement from its inception. The need to interview them was pressing due to the rapid attrition of this cohort as they approach their seventies and eighties.

Theoretical Lenses

This Element's analysis of the movement engages Stark's (1996) model of ten propositions that outline the conditions necessary for a religious movement to succeed or fail. This serves as a useful framework by which to assess the Hare Krishna movement's success so far and to predict future success or failure based on its current trajectory. Key to this theory is tension – "the degree of distinctiveness, separation, and antagonism between a religious group and the 'outside' world" (Stark and Finke, 2000, p. 127). This tension has characterized the movement's relationship with its host communities since its inception and it will be unpacked with reference to some of Stark's propositions. Stark's model emphasizes the importance of cultural continuity with the host culture and we can observe varying degrees of cultural continuity of the Hare Krishna movement with its host cultures throughout its history. This model will be used as a theoretical lens throughout this Element.

The model of alignment processes (Snow et al., 1986; Bromley and Melton, 2012; Eidson et al., 2017) provides a useful theoretical framework for understanding the movement's path since its inception in 1966. Frame alignment has been used by scholars of religion to understand the ways in which people become and remain members of religious organizations. Snow et al. (1986, p. 464) defines frame alignment as the phenomenon of congruence and complementarity between individual interests, values, and beliefs, and social movement activities, goals, and ideology. The term "frame" is derived from Goffman (1974, p. 21) who defined it as "schemata of interpretation" that enable individuals to identify and label occurrences they encounter and thereby render them meaningful. In this way, frames organize experience and guide action, on individual and collective levels. Frame alignment is necessary for participation in a movement; a movement's members work to align the interests, values, and beliefs of potential recruits with the activities, goals, and ideology of the movement. Ideological work by movement members and leaders that sustains the interest and participation of potential recruits results in successful frame alignment, which is necessary for expanding the movement's membership (Rochford, 2018, p. 36). Put another way, a social movement needs to link its master frame with the frames of potential adherents so that they may identify with the movement and participate in it (Vande Berg and Kniss, 2008, p. 90).

Frame alignment provides a way of understanding changes in the Hare Krishna movement from the 1960s up to the present in terms of the movement's placement within broader cultural contexts. It also allows us to think about the possible future paths that it may take, given the crossroads it is currently at in terms of the cultural choices being made by its membership. These choices involve those based on Indian cultural traditions as well as Western cultural expectations that are being driven by movements for equality and social justice. A number of scholars have identified the importance of the concept of frame alignment for understanding ISKCON's evolving trajectory in a changing world (Vande Berg and Kniss, 2008; Rochford, 2018; Zeller, 2021). Stark's model of cultural continuity and the frame alignment model are complementary in this analysis of the Hare Krishna movement. Frame analysis (Goffman, 1974; Snow et al., 1986; Eidson et al., 2017; Persson, 2019) will also be useful for understanding the movement's development since its inception.

Resource mobilization theory (McCarthy and Zald, 1977; Jenkins, 1983; Zald and McCarthy, 2017) also provides a useful theoretical framework for understanding the movement's changing fortunes. Resource mobilization is the process by which a group secures collective control over the resources needed for collective action (Jenkins, 1983, p. 532). Assets frequently mobilized by movements include money, facilities, labor, and legitimacy (McCarthy and Zald, 1977), as well as land, capital, and technical expertise (Tilly, 1978, p. 69, cited in Jenkins, 1983, p. 533). Tangible assets such as money, facilities, and means of communication have been distinguished from intangible or "human" assets that include specialized resources such as organizing and legal skills and the unspecialized labor of supporters (Freeman, 1979, pp. 172–5). The major issues regarding resource mobilization are the resources controlled by the group prior to mobilization efforts, the processes by which the group pools resources and directs these toward social change, and the extent to which outsiders increase the pool of resources (Jenkins, 1983, pp. 532–3).

In addition, the Element will utilize the theoretical frame of lived religion (Hall, 1997; Orsi, 2002), which aims to capture followers' everyday experiences of their religious tradition, acknowledging that religious experience often defies categorization (McGuire, 2008). To that end, emic language and spelling of unique words will be used, rather than the language of the disciplines that study the Gaudiya Vaishnava tradition, to accurately reflect the experience and practice of Hare Krishna devotees. The emic perspective is an account of the informant's own descriptions, while the etic perspective is the observer's attempt to redescribe that information (McCutcheon, 1999, p. 17). The Roman transliteration of Sanskrit terms will reflect popular pronunciation within the movement, and avoid the use of diacritical marks in Sanskrit terms, to make the Element accessible to a nonspecialist readership. It should be noted that there are variations in Roman transliteration of Sanskrit terms and one variant for each term has been chosen for consistency, except in the case of direct quotations. Hare Krishna devotees who have taken initiation receive a "spiritual name" with a suffix for men – *das* (servant) – and for women – *dasi* (servant) or *devi dasi* (divine servant). There is variation in how each individual spells this suffix – i.e. *das, dasa, Das, Dasa, dasi, Dasi, devi dasi, Devi Dasi*. The name will be spelled in the way that the name holder spells it and this will give rise to some inconsistency in spelling. In addition, in-text references will include the name plus the suffix, to honor the convention that Hare Krishna devotees always add the suffix when using their name – an acknowledgment that they think of themselves as a servant of Krishna. The same is true for names of renunciates that end in the suffixes Swami and Goswami, which indicate one who masters their senses.

Overview of the Element

This Element discusses the movement's history and early challenges as well as those that the movement currently faces against the backdrop of social, cultural, and political changes that are taking place globally. It has been constructed to give the newcomer the best possible understanding of a diverse and constantly changing religious movement. In pursuit of that goal, Section 2 discusses the beliefs and practices of followers of the movement while acknowledging the many and varied ways in which devotees follow the precepts of the tradition. Section 3 examines institutional and community dynamics and the impact these have had on the trajectory of the movement. Section 4 looks at controversies, issues, and challenges that have beset the movement since its inception as well as the ways in which members of the movement have responded to these challenges. Finally, Section 5 concludes by drawing together the main themes, reflecting upon the state of play in the movement, looking to future paths that the movement may take, and what that may tell us about its fate. I will now turn to discussing the beliefs and practices that form the bedrock of the Hare Krishna movement, while taking into account the ways in which these practices have changed to adapt to an ever-changing global context and digital world.

2 Beliefs and Practices

In this section, the main theological beliefs of the Gaudiya Vaishnava tradition that underpin the Hare Krishna movement are discussed, as well as the practices and rituals that support and enact these beliefs. It is important to note that not all devotees in the movement follow all the practices all the time. In these cases, conceptualizing adherents as participants in a movement rather than as members of an institution allows us to comprehend the different types and levels of involvement in this tradition. While these practices form the core for serious practitioners within the Gaudiya Vaishnava tradition, the reality within the Hare Krishna movement is that they will be practiced with varying degrees of regularity and strictness or may not be practiced at all by some participants in the movement. For this reason, this section adopts a lived religion approach (Hall, 1997; Orsi, 2002), which aims to understand the way adherents live and experience the tradition in their everyday lives and acknowledges that they do not always fit into neat categories (McGuire, 2008). In this way, in addition to presenting the ideal according to the tradition's precepts, the reality of adherents' lives is interrogated. With this caveat in mind, I will explore the beliefs and practices of participants in the Hare Krishna movement.

The geographical diversity of ISKCON centers also undermines broad generalization. The movement has a presence in North America, South America,

Europe, the Middle East, Asia, Asia Pacific, and Africa. This presence consists of physical infrastructure in the form of 398 temples, 88 rural communities, 109 restaurants, 176 centers, and 16 educational centers. With regard to ISKCON programs based in the community, these include 208 congregational communities (*nama hattas, bhakti vriksas, sangas*), 15 youth groups, and 15 college centers (ISKCON, 2016b). Of course, these are official ISKCON centers, and the Hare Krishna movement extends well beyond this infrastructure. Thus, both individual and institutional variety challenge popular and scholarly stereotypes.

Foundational Beliefs and Practices of the Gaudiya Vaishnava Tradition

Gaudiya Vaishnavism is a monotheistic tradition, whose adherents (Gaudiya Vaishnavas) believe in one God – Krishna; a person who worships Krishna or Vishnu is referred to as a Vaishnava.[9] The purpose of their practice is to develop pure love for Krishna by serving him and meditating on him continually. Practitioners endeavor to attain this goal by following a set of regulated practices, called *sadhana-bhakti* – "devotional service in the preliminary stage of regulated practice" (Prabhupada, 2012, p. 384). *Sadhana-bhakti* is usually simply called *sadhana*. Members of ISKCON who take formal initiation from a guru vow to follow four regulative principles of abstinence from eating meat, intoxication, gambling, and sex (except for the purpose of procreation within marriage). This is based on the belief that gratification of the senses – material activity – is a distraction from serious spiritual practice and attaining pure love for Krishna.

The purpose of the practice of *sadhana* is to attain Krishna consciousness, which is to think of Krishna, the supreme God, twenty-four hours a day. The practices are usually referred to in the movement's proselytizing materials as "*bhakti* yoga," "the yoga of devotion," or more commonly "devotional service" and "Krishna consciousness."[10] The goal is to meditate on Krishna at all times, including at the time of death when such absorption in thought of Krishna means one's spirit will be transferred to Krishna's planet – Krishnaloka – and never return to *samsara*, the cycle of birth and death (Bryant and Ekstrand, 2004, p. 445). Devotees will often refer to these processes and practices as being important for "making spiritual advancement," which refers to increasing absorption in Krishna consciousness. Underpinning these beliefs is the idea that all living beings are not their material bodies, but rather, they are the *atman* – an eternal nonmaterial soul

---

[9] Vishnu is considered by Hare Krishna devotees to be an expansion of Krishna but, for all practical purposes, the same as Krishna.

[10] Yoga can be translated as "any spiritual path leading to union with the divine" (Bryant and Ekstrand, 2004, p. 446).

that animates living bodies. Having knowledge of one's true identity is what Prabhupada referred to as "self-realization" – understanding one's identity to be that of an eternal soul (Prabhupada, 2010, p. 139). Most importantly, in addition to being an eternal soul, spiritual in nature, one is eternally "part and parcel" of Krishna (God) according to Vedic texts such as the *Varaha Purana* (Prabhupada, 2010, p. 194).

The Nectar of Devotion is Prabhupada's translation of the Vaishnava text *Bhakti-rasamrta-sindhu* and it became a prominent text of study within the movement on how to practice *bhakti* yoga. The text outlines the sixty-four ways in which a Vaishnava can carry out devotional service (Prabhupada, 2012, p. 54). According to the text, the five most important ways of practicing devotional service are: chanting Hare Krishna; studying scripture; worshipping the deity of Krishna; associating with and serving devotees of Krishna; and attending the temple of Krishna or making a temple for Krishna in one's home. Prabhupada's translation of the Vaishnava text *Upadesamrta* is *The Nectar of Instruction*. This text provides direction on how to carry out devotional service including prohibitions such as: avoiding the association with worldly minded persons who are not devotees of Krishna; refraining from eating more than necessary or collecting more funds than needed; not striving for mundane things that are difficult to obtain; and not talking about mundane subject matters (Prabhupada, 2011, Text 3).

Integral to the tradition and its preservation is the concept of *parampara* – a succession of gurus passing down spiritual knowledge (Broo, 2003, p. 281). In the *parampara*, tradition is passed on in the form of texts, and teachings are passed on from teacher to student. Taking guidance from a spiritual teacher, a guru, is regarded as necessary for being able to engage in devotional service according to Rupa Goswami (1493–1564) in his work *Bhakti-rasamrta-sindhu*, translated by Prabhupada in a summary translation (Prabhupada, 2012, p. 70). Rupa Goswami advised aspiring Vaishnavas of the necessity of "accepting the shelter of a bona fide spiritual master, taking initiation from him and serving him with respect and reverence" (Prabhupada, 2012, p. 54). The *Bhagavad Gita* also extols the virtues of following the guidance of the guru in chapter 4, verse 32: "Just try to learn the truth by approaching a spiritual master. Inquire from him submissively and render service unto him. The self-realized souls can impart knowledge unto you because they have seen the truth" (Prabhupada, 2010). This key verse in the *Bhagavad Gita* underscores the importance of seeking out, learning from, and serving the guru. The importance of the guru within the Gaudiya Vaishnava tradition sets the foundation for the centrality of the guru within ISKCON.

It is expected that devotees living in the temple ashram will take instruction and formal initiation from a guru. At the first initiation the devotee vows to follow the four regulative principles and chant the Hare Krishna mantra, counted on a set of beads, sixteen times.[11] This repetition of mantras is known as *japa* and takes about two hours. Some initiates may also take what is called "second initiation" or "*brahmanical* initiation." This involves receiving the *Gayatri* mantra from the guru, which must be silently chanted in the early morning, midday, and early evening. This initiation allows the initiate to engage in direct devotional service to the temple deities, including service on the altar and cooking food offerings for the deities.

In addition to taking guidance from a guru and repeating mantras, reading of sacred scripture is an important practice for devotees. In the Gaudiya Vaishnava tradition, the collection of texts known as the Vedas are considered to be the best source of knowledge about the nature of reality.[12] Although there are key texts within the tradition, Prabhupada emphasized that only a few need to be consulted for successful spiritual practice. He translated a set of texts from Sanskrit, and in some cases Bengali, and provided commentaries on each verse. The texts most emphasized for daily study are: *Bhagavad Gita; The Nectar of Devotion*; *Srimad-Bhagavatam* (a translation of the *Bhagavata Purana*); *The Nectar of Instruction*; *Sri Isopanisad*; and *Sri Chaitanya Charitamrta*, which is a multivolume account of the life of the sixteenth-century saint, Chaitanya, by Krishna dasa Kaviraja Goswami.

The impact that *shastras* (Vedic texts) have on epistemological and ontological concerns for participants in the Hare Krishna movement cannot be overstated, for they give rise to a different worldview than that experienced in mainstream society. *Shastras* cover an array of topics including the pastimes of Krishna and his associates, hagiographies, the nature and structure of the universe, the best way to organize society, diet and hygiene, relations between women and men, marriage, child-rearing, and education. The underlying

---

[11] The Hare Krishna mantra is a repetition of three names of God – Hare, Krishna, and Rama – in the following form: *Hare Krishna Hare Krishna Krishna Krishna Hare Hare Hare Rama Hare Rama Rama Rama Hare Hare.*

[12] *Veda* refers to sacred knowledge, and the Vedas are the oldest texts of India, compiled between ca. 1500 BCE and ca. 500–400 BCE. They contain knowledge that was heard by sages as a revelation and are therefore called *Sruti* – that which is heard. Texts after this period are not considered as part of the Vedas by Indologists, and are called *Smrti* – that which is learned (Witzel, 2003, p. 68). However, South Asian traditions also accept the later *Smrti* texts as being part of the Vedas. This is found in its most radical form in *Gaudiya Vaishnavism*. Das (1996) points out that there are different understandings among scholars regarding which texts the rubric of Veda encompasses; similarly, the associated term, Vedic, is subject to a multiplicity of interpretations in wider scholarship, as well as in the writings of Prabhupada and his followers. For the sake of a nonspecialist readership, Vedic can be defined at its most basic level as the period in Indian society when the Vedas were composed. However, in its broader, more common usage, it refers to culture and knowledge derived from the Vedas. Taking a more theological stance, Prabhupada defined Vedic as sacred knowledge and laws given by the Lord (Das, 1996).

conviction is that the best source of knowledge is from the *shastras* as they are revealed by God to self-realized souls. They are considered to be a better source of truth than secular books and science which, Prabhupada argued, were always changing, whereas Vedic knowledge is timeless and stays the same. *Shastras*, along with the self-realized guru, are thus considered to be the best authority, which by extension means that other sources of authority – such as governments or world leaders – are afforded less trust and respect. This has sometimes led to contentious relationships when devotees have interacted with the power structures of mainstream society.

Both men and women can live in the temple quarters, known as the ashram. The idea is to lead a monastic life fully devoted to the service of Krishna and ISKCON's mission as a preaching movement. For most temple residents, this will be a temporary stay that may last weeks, months, and sometimes years. Most temple residents will move out after a period of time to either pursue an occupation, marry and raise a family, or pursue university studies. The instruction to avoid nondevotees – sometimes referred to as *karmis* (people working for material rather than spiritual benefits) – has led to a sense of deliberate separation from those not involved in the movement, apart from cases where someone could be a candidate for conversion through proselytizing efforts. However, with the shift from an ashram-based movement to a congregation-based movement, the sense of estrangement from members of mainstream society has lessened, as devotees have taken on jobs and pursued higher education in mainstream society and, in many cases, sent their children to mainstream schools (Rochford, 2007a).

A Typical Day in the Temple

The temple is a key focus of activity in the Hare Krishna movement. Within the main temple building is the temple room which contains an altar with deities that are offered worship (See Figure 2). The deity is considered to be a form of God – Krishna. The temple room also houses a life-sized *murti* (form) of Prabhupada and it is also offered daily worship in the form of bathing, dressing, and food offerings. The temple is thus considered a sacred space and as such no shoes are worn in that space or within the temple building. Some devotees will be engaged in altar service for worshipping the deities. This service is restricted to devotees who have been initiated twice, with the second initiation being "*brahmanical* initiation" which qualifies one as a *pujari* (priest or priestess). Only devotees who are *brahmanas* and who are ritually pure are allowed to set foot on the altar and engage in this service. This service typically begins at 4 a.m. with the waking of the deities who have been put to rest the evening before. The waking of the deities follows a ritualized pattern of offering items

Figure 2 *Pujari* offering *arati* to the deities at Bhaktivedanta Manor, United Kingdom. Photo by Phillipe Lissac. Getty Images.

for the pleasure of the deities, such as water and sweets. Small deities will have been placed in small beds while larger deities will remain on the altar and will be awakened ritually using mantras. This is in preparation for the opening of the curtains on the altar at 4.30 a.m. for the *mangala-arati* – the auspicious *arati* – as this time is considered the most propitious time of the day for spiritual activities. *Arati* is worshipping the deity by offering items including water, flowers, incense, ghee lamps, *chamara* (yak tail whisk), and a peacock feather fan.

All other temple residents not engaged in altar service are expected to rise by 4 a.m. daily to bathe and dress in clean clothes before attending the morning program, which includes the five most potent forms of devotional service. Resident and congregational devotees gather in the temple room for the *mangala-arati* and chant the *Gurvastakam* (eight prayers to the guru) to the accompaniment of musical instruments including *karatalas* (small hand cymbals), *mridanga* (drum) and sometimes a harmonium. The altar curtains will typically close at 5 a.m., and devotees scheduled for service will engage in bathing and dressing the deities in new outfits, complete with jewelry and flower garlands. For all other temple residents and any visitors, the next part of the morning program is "*japa* time" where devotees chant sixteen rounds of *japa* on their beads, a requirement for all initiated devotees and temple residents. This is followed by deity greeting, often at 7 a.m., when the curtains of the altar are parted to reveal the deities freshly bathed and dressed in a new outfit. Deity greeting is carried out to the accompaniment of a recording of devotional prayers sung to music, most often the "Govindam Prayers" from the Vaishnava text *Brahma-samhita*, while a *pujari* offers *arati* to the deities. This is followed by *guru-puja* – the offering of items of worship to the *murti* of Prabhupada and prayers in honor of the guru in *kirtan* – call and response style group chanting of devotional prayers and songs to the accompaniment of musical instruments. Finally, there is a class based on a *shastra* (usually the *Srimad-Bhagavatam*) delivered by a devotee "in good standing" (a devotee strictly following the rules and regulations of the tradition) or a visiting guru. There may be small variations in the timing and order of the morning program from temple to temple.

The morning program is followed by breakfast, which can be anything from cooked oats, caffeine-free tea, and fruits to *kichri* (spiced rice, lentils, and vegetables), or even pizza and cake on special occasions or if a congregation member is sponsoring the meal. After breakfast, temple residents and congregation members go their separate ways to engage in their daily activities. Even large temples will then transition to a slower tempo from the morning's busy schedule of activities. The rhythm will continue in a series of regulated time periods based on the temple's deity worship schedule. Depending on the size of the temple, food and *arati* will be offered to the deities at 4 a.m., 7 a.m., lunchtime, in the afternoon at around 4 p.m., and once or twice in the evening. Visiting congregation members may stay a while after the morning program to finish chanting their rounds or depart to start work at a paid job. Temple residents will begin their designated *seva* (service) for the day, and congregation members will also fit in *seva* around other responsibilities such as work and childcare. Devotees scheduled for cleaning duty will remove and wash the serving containers and kitchen utensils and clean the common areas of the temple, including the temple room. Others may be engaged in kitchen *seva*, including cutting vegetables, cooking food for the temple's residents and visitors, and offering it to Krishna, so that it becomes sanctified food (*prasadam*). Others will engage in proselytization in public spaces in the form of *harinam sankirtan* – group chanting the names of Krishna to music (see Figures 3 and 4) – and distributing scriptural texts and other Krishna-conscious books and magazines on the street – referred to as *sankirtan* or book distribution (see Figure 5).

If the temple has a day school (*gurukula*), students and teachers will commence their lessons for the day. The *gurukula* is where children of devotees receive their education and devotees run the school as teachers and teaching assistants. Most temples have a flower garden which is used to provide flowers for the deity worship, and these are picked daily and made into garlands to be

Figure 3 Devotees performing *kirtan* at Union Square, New York City, United States, October 23, 2015. Photo by Juan Moñino. Getty Images.

Figure 4 Devotees performing *kirtan* at MardiGrass, Nimbin, New South Wales, Australia, September 18, 2022. Photo by P. Derrett. Getty Images.

Figure 5 Devotee distributing books in Nakuri, Kenya, April 3, 2022. Photo by James Wakibia/SOPA Images/LightRocket via Getty Images.

offered each morning. Some temples, including those located on farms, have a vegetable garden that needs to be cultivated and harvested. Some rural temple communities have a cow protection program designed to demonstrate that cows should not be killed for their meat but, instead, looked after in exchange for their milk. To that end, the temple's herd of cows is fed, milked, and cared for by devotees trained in looking after them. Some temples, particularly those in built-up urban areas, such as London and Los Angeles, have a temple shop that sells devotional paraphernalia including small deities, incense, books, recorded lectures, and clothing. Temple shops often serve as a space for devotees to congregate and catch up with each other. Some temples have a restaurant that is open to the public for the purpose of distributing sanctified food, which needs to be staffed.

Lunch and an evening meal will be served for the temple residents and visitors. There may be an evening class given in the temple room, based on a scriptural text such as the *Bhagavad Gita*. When there is no festival being held, devotees may attend the evening *arati*; if they have free time, they will spend it reading scripture, listening to audio classes of Prabhupada or other ISKCON gurus, spending time with other devotees, or tending to personal needs. It is expected that temple residents retire to bed reasonably early so that they can rise by 4 a.m. for the morning program. Visiting gurus, who are mostly *sannyasis*, travel the world to preach and visit temples, giving classes, and meeting with their disciples, and this will give rise to more visitors and activity, as will holy days and festivals. Home programs, where a congregation member hosts devotees in their home, consist of a class given by a visiting guru or other senior devotee, *kirtan*, and a feast.

Congregational Life

The rather regulated and idealized representation of what happens within the temple, which is a monastic environment, starts to break down when we move away from the temple as a focus of activity. It is here that adherence to these ideal standards becomes less certain, because obedience to a set of principles and practices is self-regulated, whereas temple residents lead a monastic life and live under the direction of temple authorities. Former residents who are married, sometimes with children, are referred to as *grihasthas* (householders). There are also Indian congregation members, most of whom have not taken initiation. It is expected as a norm, but certainly not regulated and policed, that devotees who live in their own homes will arrange their home to engage in devotional service. They may set up a shrine in the home with deities of Krishna and sometimes a *murti* of Prabhupada. They may carry out a scaled-down version of the temple morning program which includes some or all the following: offering food and other items, bathing and dressing the deities (*puja*); chanting sixteen (or fewer) rounds on beads of the Hare Krishna mantra; reading scriptures including the *Bhagavad Gita*, *Srimad-Bhagavatam*, and *The Nectar of Devotion*; and listening to recorded lectures by Prabhupada. These activities may be performed in the morning or at other times of the day, but for devotees who are engaged in paid work, it would be common to do them in the morning before work or in the evening after work. Sundays will often be set aside for visiting the temple for the Sunday feast, which consists of *kirtan*, a class, a vegetarian meal, and the opportunity to associate with other devotees. Some temples hold a Sunday school for children during the Sunday feast program.

Pilgrimage, Holy Days, and Retreats

As with all religious traditions, the Hare Krishna movement has sacred sites that are integral to the Gaudiya Vaishnava tradition. These sacred sites are called *dhams* and the most important ones are in India – Vrindavan and Govardhan in Uttar Pradesh, and Mayapura in West Bengal. Vrindavan is considered by Vaishnavas to be the childhood home of Krishna in his earthly avatar form as a cowherd boy. It is a popular place of pilgrimage, especially during the month of *Karttik* (October to November), when devotees are advised to take on extra services (Prabhupada, 2012, p. 72) because the benefits of spiritual activity are

Figure 6 Sri Sri Krishna Balaram Mandir (ISKCON Vrindavan), Vrindavan, Uttar Pradesh, India, March 5, 2012. Photo by Arterra/Universal Images. Getty Images.

said to be multiplied at this time. ISKCON has a temple (see Figure 6), guest-house, restaurant, and *gurukula* there, as well as long-term accommodation for devotees who wish to live in Vrindavan because of the spiritual benefits of living in a holy place. Govardhan and Radha Kunda are other sacred sites near Vrindavan that attract pilgrims from around the globe due to the accounts of the activities of Krishna and his divine consort and feminine counterpart, Radharani, recounted in Vaishnava texts including the *Bhagavata Purana*.

Figure 7 Temple of the Vedic Planetarium under construction at ISKCON Mayapur, Nadia, West Bengal, India, February 23, 2023. Photo by Alan Herbert.

Mayapura is thought to be the birthplace of Chaitanya, and for that reason is highly revered by Gaudiya Vaishnavas. A large swath of land near the Ganges River, also considered to be a sacred site, is owned by ISKCON. Here, devotees have built a temple, guesthouse, and restaurant, as well as residential dwellings for long-term residents who want the spiritual benefits of living in the *dham* and the community that comes along with this. At the time of writing, the Temple of the Vedic Planetarium (see Figure 7) is being constructed to showcase the Vedic conception of the cosmology of the universe as depicted in the *Bhagavata Purana* (Sri Mayapur Chandrodaya Mandir Temple of the Vedic Planetarium, 2013).

Commemorating holy days, often in the form of an *Utsava* (festival), is an important part of the Gaudiya Vaishnava tradition and is considered to be a way of maintaining enthusiasm for spiritual practice. Festivals commemorate holy days, including the appearance of Krishna's avatars on earth and their various activities, as well as the birth and death anniversaries of significant teachers in the tradition's lineage of gurus. Fasting until either noon, moonrise, or midnight is a feature of many holy days, the idea being that instead of taking the time to prepare and consume food, one's focus is on spiritual activity. Devotees

Figure 8 Bathing the deities on a festival day at ISKCON New Mayapur, Château d'Oublaisse, France, August 13, 2011. Photo by Ilya Mauter. Wikimedia Commons

meditate on the avatar or guru being honored on that day to enhance spiritual advancement (see Figure 8). Festivals vary in scale and prominence, and some festivals draw bigger crowds because they attract not only Gaudiya Vaishnavas, but also Hindus who worship deities other than Krishna within the Hindu pantheon. Ekadasi is a holy day that occurs every two weeks when devotees fast from grains or fast from food entirely.

The largest festival held on temple grounds is Janmasthami, which celebrates Krishna's appearance as a blue cowherd boy in Mathura, near Vrindavan. Other festivals that celebrate the various incarnations of Krishna include Divali and Ramanavami, which are also popular Hindu festivals, Radhasthami, Balarama's appearance day, and Nrsimha Caturdasi. Prabhupada's birthday (*Vyasa-puja* – the honoring of the guru on his or her birthday or "appearance day") and the anniversary of Prabhupada's passing attract ISKCON devotees rather than the wider Indian-Hindu congregation. Festivals that celebrate the birth of prominent teachers in the disciple line include the appearance day of Bhaktisiddhanta Sarasvati Thakura (the guru of ISKCON's founder, Prabhupada) and the appearance day of Bhaktivinoda Thakura (who is also the father of Bhaktsiddhanta Sarasvati Thakura).

The biggest festival in terms of public outreach is Ratha-Yatra (see Figures 9 and 10), known in English as "the festival of the chariots" and held in every major city in the world (Rosen, 2006, p. 212). The centerpiece of the festival is the deity of Krishna in the form of Jagannatha (the lord of the universe) and his expansions – his brother Balarama and his sister Subhadra. Each deity sits atop a large cart (*ratha*) pulled with ropes by devotees along a designated path throughout the city. The festival signifies the devotee's spirit of being a humble servant of Krishna (Rosen, 2006, p. 213). The festival has its origins in Jagannatha Puri in the state of Orissa in India, and has been held in ISKCON since 1967 (Satsvarupa das Goswami, 1980b), taking place in most major cities in the world. It includes a festival known in North America as the Festival of India, which includes *kirtan*, dance and drama performances, vegetarian food, and stalls where Prabhupada's books are available for sale. The festival attracts hundreds, and sometimes thousands, of people, including devotees and members of the public.

The COVID-19 pandemic has shifted some festivals to the Internet due to restrictions on organizing mass gatherings of people in various parts of the world. In June 2020, Ratha-Yatra was moved online and touted as the world's first digital Ratha-Yatra across six continents (Loiwal, 2020). Other workarounds for Ratha-Yatra have included a drive-through *darshan* ("seeing the deities") and an online celebration organized by ISKCON Toronto in collaboration with other local

Figure 9 Ratha-Yatra festival in Paris, France. Photo by Phillipe Lissac/ Godong. Getty Images.

Figure 10 Ratha-Yatra festival in London, United Kingdom, September 4, 2022. Photo by Matthew Chattle/Future Publishing via Getty Images.

Hindu temples (Smullen, 2021b). One of the organizers described the impacts that COVID-19 had on their temple community: "Compared to the U.S., where many temples have been open with precautions for some time, in Toronto, it's been very hard . . . We haven't been able to go back to the temple – only recently have things started to open up" (Smullen, 2021b). In-person Ratha-Yatra has resumed in cities globally.

Spiritual retreats have become increasingly popular in the Hare Krishna movement for an increasingly dispersed community over the past twenty years. As devotees have left the close-knit confines of the temple ashram, or moved away from nearby houses, they have experienced less engagement with their local temple congregation, and their sense of community has become less locally focused. For these reasons, they seek association with others, especially since associating with devotees is one of the five most important forms of devotional service outlined in *The Nectar of Devotion* (Prabhupada, 2012, p. 72). Although they have the goal of fostering focused spiritual practice, retreats usually have the look and feel of a festival. The core components of retreats are *kirtan*, seminars, and workshops, as well as dance and drama performances. These occasions provide ample opportunity for reminiscing about the early days of the movement when Prabhupada was still alive, and for informally catching up with old friends and acquaintances. Popular retreats include the Festival of Inspiration held annually at the New Vrindavan farm community in West Virginia, which primarily attracts devotees from across the United States as well as devotees from other parts of the globe.

Like festivals, retreats have also been forced into virtual space due to global COVID-19 lockdowns since 2020. One retreat – Virtual Bhakti Retreat for Spanish Speakers – which had been already running online for ten years, was easily able to continue during the pandemic (Smullen, 2020). The Vrindavan Institute for Higher Education (VIHE) Govardhan retreat has been held for many years and consists of spiritual seminars and *kirtan* along with guided pilgrimages to sacred sites in Govardhan, near Vrindavan. Due to the COVID-19 pandemic, the retreat was moved online in 2020 and plans to return to a face-to-face event in 2023 (VIHE, 2023). There are also specialized forums where gurus gather with their disciples. Some spiritual retreats are aimed at proselytizing newcomers and use the medium of a yoga retreat to that end. In still other forums, devotees attend festivals organized by other groups, such as the Burning Man Festival in Nevada, where they perform *kirtan* and distribute books and *prasadam*.

Conclusion

The beliefs and practices of the Hare Krishna movement have their roots in the Gaudiya Vaishnava tradition and have been adapted for a global and Western cultural context. Although the rationale for these beliefs and practices can be traced to scriptural texts, the reality of their manifestation as lived religion is far less cut and dried, as there is variation in the way followers of the Hare Krishna movement adhere to the tenets of the Gaudiya Vaishnava tradition. This account of daily routines has attempted to provide a sense of the varying degrees of commitment by devotees to the tradition's principles and practices.

In the next section, a discussion of institutional and community dynamics will provide greater context for thinking about the diversity that is necessarily involved in adhering to principles and practices that have been adapted from another culture. As such, the discussion of institutional and community dynamics will provide another lens for thinking about how Hare Krishna devotees relate to each other in a system of relationships and networks, and how those relational networks provide a context for identity and meaning-making.

3 Institutional and Community Dynamics

The Hare Krishna movement is a phenomenon that coalesces around the hard institutional structure of the corporate entity of ISKCON. However, to restrict this discussion to ISKCON would reduce the movement to its institutional forms and processes and ignore the complexity of the community that has grown around this institutional structure. Resource mobilization theory, frame alignment, and Stark's framework for how new religions succeed provide a means for understanding the complex set of factors at play. An examination of social dynamics within the movement considers the group dynamics in the various types of Hare Krishna communities. Issues concerning identity and the concept of belonging are integral to this discussion, such as inclusion and exclusion on ideological grounds and matters of purity that surround the following of devotional vows. The question of what it means to be a devotee is considered in terms of practice, ideological stance, initiation, and community membership. Theories of frame alignment and resource mobilization are used to examine the transition from a monastic movement to a congregation-based movement and from Western-based congregations to those that are increasingly Indian-Hindu. The responses to that shift, including changes in proselytization methods, are also analyzed, and these clarify the movement's history and current situation. A discussion of the impact of the Internet and social media on Hare Krishna communities will demonstrate how online communities both enhance and disrupt relationships and other forms of community. Finally, a discussion of how the movement has been impacted by the COVID-19 pandemic provides an account of how the movement is faring in a disrupted global context.

ISKCON as the Institutional Structure of the Hare Krishna Movement

From the earliest days of his mission in the United States, Prabhupada had understood that its growth and sustainability depended on having an institutional structure. Accordingly, Prabhupada registered his fledgling movement as the International Society for Krishna Consciousness (ISKCON) in 1966 (Satsvarupa das Goswami, 1993c). The first level of management Prabhupada instituted was a temple president at each center. In the late 1960s, as ISKCON attracted many new followers and the movement expanded rapidly, Prabhupada added another layer of management when he formed a Governing Body Commission (GBC) in July 1970. This comprised twelve members appointed by Prabhupada to assist him in the management of the society. The number later expanded to twenty-four (Shinn, 1987, p. 54) and each GBC member was responsible for the management of ISKCON in a different part of the world. Apart from managing the economic and organizational aspects of ISKCON, administration of an organization guided by Prabhupada's spiritual principles also meant ensuring that the high spiritual standards he had set for his committed disciples would be followed, such as maintaining the vows taken at initiation. Although Prabhupada remained involved in overseeing the affairs of ISKCON, he increasingly delegated the management of the society to his most senior male disciples throughout the 1970s, and this was made possible by the management structure he had put in place. This enabled him to finish his translation of the *Bhagavata Purana* (Prabhupada, 1976).[13]

The core management structure that Prabhupada set up when he founded ISKCON is still in place. This includes the GBC, temple presidents, and the Bhaktivedanta Book Trust (BBT) – the publishing arm of ISKCON. Management roles within these organizational structures are divided by geographical region. Representatives of the GBC are allocated to geographical zones throughout the world, a temple president oversees the running of an individual temple, and BBT trustees are appointed to global geographical zones. In addition to these core management roles, other management roles in ISKCON include overseeing various projects, the most prominent currently being the construction of the Temple of the Vedic Planetarium in Mayapura. Other projects include Food for Life food distribution and numerous education projects and proselytization initiatives. Gurus act as spiritual leaders by providing religious guidance to the community and initiating new devotees. It is important to note that many GBC members are also gurus, thus serving a dual role of manager and spiritual teacher. After Prabhupada's death in 1977, ISKCON immediately began the task of surviving the difficult period after a founder's death while engaged in a period of collective grief and mourning. Eleven disciples took over the spiritual leadership of ISKCON by taking the role of gurus. This topic will be taken up in Section 4, since it has been one of the most controversial issues in the movement's history. After Prabhupada's passing, the focus of ISKCON's members became one of institutional survival (Squarcini, 2000).

While it is important to examine the institutional and governance structure of ISKCON, it is equally important to understand what defines ISKCON as an organization, and what defines the broader Hare Krishna movement beyond this formal institutional structure. O'Connell (2019) has conceptualized the Gaudiya Vaishnava tradition in terms of hard, medium, and soft institutions. Hard institutions have a system of centralized and coercive authority; medium institutions have diverse and diffuse networks of affiliation, especially through groups of gurus and disciples; and soft institutions comprise mainly symbolic means of engaging in the worship of Krishna. O'Connell argues that the Gaudiya Vaishnava tradition has, for most of its history, been based on soft and medium institutions, rarely tending toward hard institutions until the

---

[13] Prabhupada's translation of the *Bhagavata Purana* is called the *Srimad-Bhagavatam*.

formation of the Gaudiya Math by Bhaktisiddhanta in the early twentieth century. As the tradition matured, the medium and soft institutional structures became more prominent, and the hard institutional structures less so (O'Connell, 2019). Understanding the nature of medium institutions lies at the heart of the distinction between ISKCON as an institution and the broader Hare Krishna movement.

The Role of Migration

The genesis and expansion of the Hare Krishna movement has relied upon migration. Prabhupada was instructed by his guru as early as 1922 to preach Krishna consciousness in the West, and Prabhupada understood the instruction to mean traveling to Western countries to spread the teachings of Krishna consciousness (Greene, 2016, pp. 18, 38). In 1965, the United States government passed the Immigration and Nationality Act, which opened the country to increased numbers of immigrants who were more diverse in terms of their country of origin, ethnicity, and religious faith (Lawrence, 2002; Hatton, 2015; Orchowski, 2015). Prabhupada was one of many Indian swamis who traveled to the United States after its immigration laws were changed (Shinn, 1987, p. 38). As he set sail on the *Jaladuta* in August 1965 (Greene, 2016, p. 77) the process of immigration that would be integral to spreading the Hare Krishna movement was set in motion. As a new immigrant in the United States, Prabhupada attracted a following which then branched out to San Francisco and other parts of the country (Satsvarupa das Goswami, 1993b). In the next stage of the movement's expansion, he sent three couples to the United Kingdom in 1969 (Satsvarupa das Goswami, 1980a) and they became ISKCON's next migrants.

The first devotees went to India with Prabhupada in 1970 (Greene, 2016, p. 213), initiating a trend of Western devotees traveling to India on pilgrimage to Vaishnava holy sites. In some cases they moved to India on a long-term basis to establish temples in Vrindavan and Mayapura, as well as other cities. Since then, Western devotees have continued to migrate to Indian holy sites, impelled by the belief that living in the holy *dham* enhances spiritual practice and spiritual growth. Today, there is a community of devotees living in Vrindavan, as well as a large community of Western devotees in Mayapura. Thus, the movement of ideas and culture from India to the United States was carried by processes of migration that branched out across the globe and circled back to their point of origin, transformed by their adaptation by new host cultures.

In the 1970s and 1980s, when ISKCON was at the peak of its growth and expansion, it was common for devotees to move from their country of origin to other countries to serve the mission and open new ISKCON centers. In addition to being instrumental in allowing Prabhupada to establish his Western mission, changes in immigration law in the United States in 1965 also led to an increase in Indian-Hindus migrating to the United States (Rochford, 2007a, p. 182). From 1990 to 2000, the number of Indians living in the United States doubled to over 1.6 million (Vande Berg and Kniss, 2008, p. 80). Since the Second World War Indians have migrated to Europe, North America, Australia, and New Zealand due to the demand for skilled labor and the relaxation of immigration laws, and they have found places to worship in their adopted countries (Sinha, 2019, p. 182). Because ISKCON has temples in many countries globally it has attracted many Indian-Hindu immigrants. As a result, the global presence of ISKCON centers, coupled with constant movement by devotees across inter-national borders to serve in ISKCON temples, has resulted in "transnational flow" (Vande Berg and Kniss, 2008, p. 85).

The migration of the movement's members around the globe involves a complex process of cultural exchange. Prabhupada introduced aspects of Indian culture in his delivery of the teachings of Krishna consciousness to his first American disciples. As the movement expanded, it was not only the Indian cultural aspects that were transported but also the Western and specifically American adaptation of them that was imported into new host cultures. This effect was blunted in host cultures that had significant Indian-Hindu populations and Hindu cultures, includ-ing African countries such as Kenya, Asian countries including Malaysia, and Fiji. The complexity of migration flows and their impacts on local cultures within the Hare Krishna movement is echoed in broader scholarly research. In a study of transnational religion, Ebaugh (2004) observed that two-way communication across borders, along with regular travel in both directions, promoted religious innovation both in the United States and in immigrants' countries of origin. This phenomenon can be observed in the Hare Krishna movement as a transnational religious movement that has been driven by migration.

Believing without Belonging

It is useful at this point to expand on the difference between ISKCON as an institution and the Hare Krishna movement since it addresses issues of belonging and identity. Utilizing the terms "ISKCON" and "Hare Krishna movement" is not straightforward and uniform but is, rather, context-dependent. Understanding this requires us to consider the terms that adherents use in relation to themselves and other adherents. The concept of emic (insider) perspective and etic (outsider) perspective (McCutcheon, 1999, p. 17) will be useful in gaining this comprehen-sion. "Hare Krishna" can be thought of as etic language – a term used by outsiders to refer to an adherent of the Gaudiya Vaishnava tradition outside India. "Devotee" and "Vaishnava" are terms used by adherents to refer to each other and are therefore emic, or insider language. "Member of ISKCON" is a phrase that is used less often and would be used by insiders and outsiders to refer to a person who identifies with belonging to the institution of ISKCON.

While some devotees consider themselves to be members of ISKCON, others would reject that identification. This could be for a few reasons. First, it may be that they formally left the institution of ISKCON and, in some cases, joined another Gaudiya Vaishnava organization. Second, an individual may have simply drifted away from regular or irregular participation at ISKCON temples for a variety of reasons, including family and work demands. Others may still participate in ISKCON services and events but not identify with being a member of the institution. The fluidity of these categorizations is compounded by the fact that ISKCON has never systematically and consistently kept records of membership, thus blurring the distinction between belonging and not belonging. In all these cases, the identification is with being a devotee of Krishna, which, in some adherents' understanding, transcends affiliation with a religious institution. It should therefore be clear that in cases where affiliation with ISKCON has been maintained, ISKCON and the Hare Krishna movement would be synonymous. In cases where affiliation with ISKCON has either weakened or been completely severed, but the identification as a devotee of Krishna remains, the conceptualization of the Hare Krishna movement could include some combination of ISKCON, other Gaudiya Vaishnava groups, and the complex network of devotee relationships.

It should be clear, therefore, that some devotees of Krishna have a belief in the principles of Krishna consciousness without feeling that they belong to a religious institution. Davie (1990) argues that increasing numbers of people have religious belief without belonging to a religious institution in any meaningful sense. This would be the case with devotees of Krishna who maintain belief in the principles of Krishna consciousness without interaction with the institution of ISKCON and other devotees, or who interact with other devotees but do not interact with the institution of ISKCON. As devotees find online spaces to connect, this trend toward identifying more with a community than a religious organization is enhanced. The COVID-19 pandemic accelerated this trend, as in-person services at temples and festivals were suspended and moved online.

Apostasy, Defection, and Schism

As early as 1986, concerns about apostasy were apparent when it was noted that long-standing members were leaving and that *gurukulis* – children of devotees born into the movement – were not maintaining a Krishna-conscious culture.

In emic language, devotees were "blooping" or "fringing out" (Shukavak Dasa, 1986, p. 41).[14] ISKCON members who left the organization in the 1980s and 1990s were either practicing Krishna consciousness at home or forming communities of similarly disaffected devotees. In some cases, they joined other Gaudiya Vaishnava groups (Rochford, 2009, pp. 281–2). As a result, ISKCON experienced a significant exodus of members to other Gaudiya Vaishnava groups beginning in the 1990s. These groups include devotee communities based on private ownership of adjoining land, Gaudiya Vaishnava groups such as those led by Sridhara Maharaja and Narayana Maharaja (both now deceased), and groups headed by gurus who have left ISKCON.

In 1987, the GBC expelled one of the original eleven gurus, Kirtanananda Swami (1937–2011; also known by his honorific title, Bhaktipada), from ISKCON due to serious criminal acts that had occurred within his jurisdiction at the New Vrindaban farm community in West Virginia. The GBC also maintained that he had created institutions controlled by himself alone, thus creating a movement separate from ISKCON (ISKCON Governing Body Commission, 1987). In 1988, New Vrindaban and its satellite temples and centers were removed from ISKCON, due to not following GBC directives of 1987 that forbade Kirtanananda Swami from participating in the functions of ISKCON (ISKCON Governing Body Commission, 1988). Kirtanananda was convicted of racketeering and mail fraud violations in 1993. He was indicted with conspiracy to murder, but was not convicted on that charge, although another member of the community was charged with murder (US Court of Appeals for the Fourth Circuit, 1993). Kirtanananda was imprisoned in 1996 (Associated Press, 1996) after being sentenced to twelve years, but was released after eight years due to failing health. He died in India in 2004 (Fox, 2011). New Vrindaban was readmitted to ISKCON in 1998 (New Vrindaban, 2021a).

While defections from ISKCON to other organizations have been frequent, schism has been less common. Schisms involve the breaking away of a group from an organization to form a new one (Lewis and Lewis, 2009, p. 2). The first major schism within ISKCON occurred in 1982 when one of the original eleven

---

[14] From ISKCON'S earliest days in 1966, the term "blooping" came to signify a devotee leaving the practice of Krishna consciousness. The term originated from a devotee who was inspired by Prabhupada's lectures, which regularly included the metaphor of falling back into the material illusory ocean of *maya* (illusion). When discussing a devotee who had left the practice of Krishna consciousness, the devotee made the gesture of throwing a stone and making the sound "bloop." After that, every time a devotee left Krishna consciousness, devotees would say that the person had "blooped" (Achyutananda Das, 2012, p. 75). "Fringing out" was a term used from ISKCON's early days to refer to those who were not considered to be serious full-time devotees, often signified by not moving into the temple ashram, or moving out of the temple ashram and visiting as a congregational member. Thus, there was a clear distinction between belonging and not belonging.

gurs, Jayatirtha, left with his disciples (Rochford, 2009, p. 269). It became common knowledge in 1980 that Jayatirtha was having problems following the vows necessary for his position as guru and GBC member in ISKCON. The crisis came to a head at GBC meeting in Mayapura in 1982, when Jayatirtha's association with one of Prabhupada's godbrothers, Sridhar Maharaja, became a cause for concern for the GBC.[15] Sridhar Maharaja had been a source of advice to ISKCON's successor gurus shortly after Prabhupada's death, but he had since been blamed for giving advice that was perceived as damaging to ISKCON; consequently, ISKCON's leadership saw him as an enemy. The GBC ordered Jayatirtha to cease associating with Sridhar Maharaja, but he refused. Instead, he made a decision to go to Sridhar Maharaja's *math* just across the river in Navadvipa and to take his disciples, who were nearby in Mayapura at that time, with him.[16] The GBC attempted to stop Jayatirtha's disciples and other disciples of Prabhupada from going with him and effectively leaving ISKCON, but were only partially successful (Vicitravirya das, personal communication, 2003).

Another schism that ISKCON has faced is the ISKCON Revival Movement (IRM), formed in 2000 as a pressure group to revive and reform ISKCON based on a particular interpretation of Prabhupada's instructions on succession (Jones and Ryan, 2006, p. 199). Rochford (2009, p. 274) categorizes the IRM as both a schismatic and an insurgent group, because its mission is to replace ISKCON's religious authority structure with Prabhupada as ISKCON's only initiating guru. Composed of ISKCON devotees from all over the world, IRM is based on a belief that the spiritual purity and prestige of ISKCON has undergone a deterioration since the passing of Prabhupada. It "seeks to restore ISKCON to its former glory, purity and philosophical chastity through the re-institution of all the instructions and standards that Srila Prabhupada gave, beginning with his role as the sole authority and diksa [initiating] guru for ISKCON" (ISKCON Revival Movement, 2022d). The movement has an active website, where it publishes newsletters and papers that present the *ritvik* doctrine that Prabhupada is the only legitimate guru in ISKCON (ISKCON Revival Movement, 2022a).[17] A Facebook page and Twitter accounts provide updates on its activities, which include distributing literature at ISKCON temples and festivals. The Facebook page has over 6,000 followers and the Twitter account has over 1,300 followers (ISKCON Revival Movement, 2022b; ISKCON Revival Movement, 2022c).

---

[15] A godbrother is a man who has the same guru as oneself. A godsister is a woman who has the same guru as oneself.
[16] A *math* is a monastic institution.
[17] The *rivik* doctrine will be discussed further in Section 3.

Although scholars often assume that defection, factionalism, and schism rob a movement of its energy and vitality (Rochford, 2009, p. 282), if social movements are seen as fluid, then organizational boundaries become less important than the broader contexts in which movements operate (Gusfield, 1981, p. 323). In this way, Prabhupada's teachings and authority have found new life found beyond the institutional borders of ISKCON (Rochford, 2009, p. 283). Such an acknowledgment is important considering the ever-increasing diversity of the Hare Krishna movement. This is evidenced in the hard institutional structures outside of ISKCON in the form of other Gaudiya Vaishnava organizations, the medium institutional structures of devotee social networks and communities, and the soft institutional structures of devotional practices. The phenomena of defections, factions, and schisms exist within an institutional view of the Hare Krishna movement, where ISKCON is seen as equivalent to the movement. If a distinction between the institution and the broader Hare Krishna movement is entertained, these phenomena can be seen as evidence of diversity and differentiation within the movement.

Transition From a Monastic Movement to a Congregation-Based Movement

In the 1960 and 1970s, being a member of ISKCON involved living a communal and monastic life in the temple ashram and living a life of celibacy, where interaction with the opposite sex was to be minimized if one was to make any progress in achieving full Krishna consciousness. This expectation was not realistic for some devotees, and Prabhupada made it clear that the only option for appropriately satisfying sexual desire was marriage where it could be engaged in the act of procreation. As a result, a number of devotees started asking Prabhupada for permission to marry as early as late 1965 (Rochford, 2007a, pp. 54–8). By the 1980s, greater numbers of devotees transitioned from living a single and celibate life in the ashram to marrying and raising a family. Finding paid employment was essential for funding this lifestyle shift. During the 1980s, the number of married householders with children increased dramatically among ISKCON members in the United States. This meant that although there were members who remained single and lived a monastic life in the ashram, rendering full-time service, they were no longer the majority within ISKCON. The institution had thus transitioned from a predominantly monastic, ashram-based movement to a householder-based movement (Rochford, 2007a, pp. 61–2, 70–1). Madsen (2000) observes that the phenomenon of *grihasthas* moving away from the temple also occurred in Nordic countries, nations in the former Soviet Union, and the United Kingdom. The transition from temple life to congregation life took place in Slovenia about ten years later than in North America, starting in the late 1990s, with participation consisting of visits to the temple and taking part in *nama hatta* and *sanga* programs – consisting of scriptural discourse and *kirtan* in devotee homes (Crnic, 2009, pp. 120–1). This shift had implications for ISKCON's economic fortunes, in terms of human labor and finances which declined dramatically throughout the 1980s, as well as its ethnic and cultural makeup.

Transition from Western-Based Congregations to Hindu-Based Congregations

Along with a large and growing presence and membership in India, ISKCON also has a growing Indian membership in Western countries. This has been accompanied by a decline in the recruitment of Westerners. From ISKCON's earliest days in the United States, Prabhupada made it clear that the Hare Krishna movement was not a Hindu movement or even a religious movement, but rather "the function of the soul" (Prabhupada, 1992, p. 1577). He avoided recruiting Indian-Hindu immigrants, as the mission given to him by his guru was dedicated to introducing Westerners to Krishna consciousness. Nevertheless, in Western nations, including the United States, ISKCON temples have become a social and religious center for Indian-Hindu immigrants (Zaidman, 2000, p. 217). The gradually increasing Indian-Hindu involvement was a relatively straightforward affair until ISKCON's leaders found it useful to leverage the movement's connection to Hinduism. This included defending ISKCON from the anticult movement in the United States by aligning itself with Hinduism in order to be considered a legitimate religious tradition (Rochford, 2007a, p. 184). Raising funds from the Indian-Hindu community after the decline in revenue streams from book distribution also proved to be a pragmatic course of action for some of ISKCON's leaders (Vande Berg and Kniss, 2008, p. 87). In the United Kingdom, resisting attempts to close Bhaktivedanta Manor over a planning dispute with local residents and the local council involved drawing on the support of the Hindu community, result-ing in a much greater Indian-Hindu presence at the temple (Nye, 1996). In 1996, the campaign was successful in keeping the temple open (Nye, 1998, pp. 430–1), and to this day it boasts a large Indian-Hindu congregation, attracting crowds in the tens of thousands on the most important festival days.

These strategic moves constituted another stage in ISKCON's resource mobilization efforts, this time drawing on the Hindu religious tradition to lay claim to a legitimacy not drawn upon by ISKCON before – that of being Hindus. This allowed ISKCON's members to reject the label and category of "new religious movement" that had been applied by scholars of religion in the 1960s and 1970s. This move had short-term benefits for several ISKCON communities and temples, but was to have long-term consequences for the movement in the United States and the United Kingdom, as well as other Western countries including Australia. As Zaidman (2000, p. 217) notes, giving political power to Indian-Hindu immigrants promoted a process of integration in the United States. As a result of these developments, the number of Indian-Hindus attending ISKCON programs and services increased throughout the 1970s and 1980s, and by the early 1990s, Indian immigrants were a significant presence within ISKCON (Zaidman, 2000). Consequently, in the 1980s and 1990s, ISKCON stabilized as a legitimate religious organization, to a large degree, due to the involvement of Indian-Hindu immigrants (Vande Berg and Kniss, 2008, p. 89). Those sections of ISKCON that had the opportunity to embrace and leverage the minority Indian-Hindu community due to the demographics of their geographical region were attempting to reduce the tension with their host culture that had manifested in the form of anticult activity.

A similar demographic shift can be observed in Western countries including the United Kingdom and Australia, but the shift to Indian-Hindu congregations documented in the United States is not uniform across the globe. For example, Leman and Roos (2007, p. 328) noted that ISKCON Belgium has no link with Hindu or other immigrant communities, except for those living in the Netherlands, and that there are not that many Indian families or other active *bhakti* movements in Belgian society. The authors acknowledged that this may change with increasing Indian immigration to Antwerp and other Belgian cities such as Brussels. A perusal of the temple's website (Radhadesh, no date) and Facebook page (Radhadesh, 2022) indicates that, in fact, there is an Indian presence in the congregation and visitors, but it is far less than can be observed in temples in the United States, United Kingdom, and Australia.

A Changing Relationship with Broader Society

Using frame alignment theory, we can identify ISKCON's master frame as Krishna consciousness and a spiritually oriented Vedic culture that supports it (Vande Berg and Kniss, 2008, p. 90). In the 1960s and early 1970s, ISKCON's members aligned the principles of Krishna consciousness with the ideals of those engaged in social movements and the counterculture. Part of this effort involved comparing the consciousness-altering effects of chanting with the highs of drug use in the counterculture community (Rochford, 2018, pp. 241–7). However, as the counterculture and political activism dropped off by the mid-1970s, so did ISKCON's recruitment. Further declines in recruitment and membership occurred as some members left after Prabhupada died in 1977 and new leadership took his place. This led to a sharp drop in book distribution and its resulting income in North America (Rochford, 2018, p. 47). The decline was to be compounded by the departure of a number of successor gurus in the early to mid-1980s. This effect was exacerbated by the fact that one of the departing gurus had made book distribution his main project. A similar effect was to ensue in Europe in the late 1990s with the departure of another of the successor gurus who also made the promotion of book distribution one of his key projects. Thus, while ISKCON's master frame of Krishna consciousness and the Vedic culture that supported it resonated with the countercultural youth of the 1960s and 1970s, increased participation of Indian-Hindus has provided a new group that can resonate with this master frame (Vande Berg and Kniss, 2008, p. 90).

While ISKCON initially rejected the frame of a Hindu movement, this alternate frame was adopted later by sections of the movement when it was convenient for resource mobilization. Not all ISKCON members are aligned with the frame of ISKCON as a Hindu movement, however, but rather align with the frame of ISKCON as a nonsectarian movement for promoting Krishna consciousness. Hence, there are competing frames that have given rise to divisions within the movement, both at a local and a global level. These competing frames become even starker in their contrast when we consider the increased prevalence of ISKCON in India and India's increased prominence in ISKCON, both in terms of membership and as a place of pilgrimage. There are 239 ISKCON centers in India (ISKCON, 2016b) and the Indian GBC holds increasing political power, weighing in on important issues including female gurus and child abuse cases, often in ways that are contrary to modern Western sensibilities. In a broader context, 79.8 percent of India's residents are Hindu (Kramer, 2021) and there is an increasing prevalence of Hindu nationalism (Chatterji, Hansen, and Jaffrelot, 2019; Shani, 2021). These contrasting frames are at the heart of questions about what forward path ISKCON should take if it wants to be relevant in a rapidly changing world.

The alignment of ISKCON with the Indian-Hindu community does not mean that the earlier frames of ISKCON as a world-transforming movement have disappeared. Online discussions among devotees reveal that Prabhupada's mission to make the world Krishna conscious still finds support in sections of the movement. Many of ISKCON's temples have become Hinduized in terms of temple resident and congregational makeup and temple and festival programs. However, a wider devotee community exists beyond the temple in social networks of friends and guru and disciple communities; these are increasingly mediated in online spaces. These communities remain diverse with a large Western component that aspires to fulfill Prabhupada's original mission.

It also needs to be acknowledged that there has been a response to the Hinduization of ISKCON's temples in the form of innovative new outreach programs, yet another form of frame alignment.

Resource Mobilization amid Changing Economic Fortunes

Stark's argument that religious movements grow to the extent that they have a highly motivated volunteer labor force, including those willing to proselytize (Stark, 1996, p. 140), is demonstrated in ISKCON's early years when it was rapidly expanding. Implicit in this proposition is the concept of resource mobilization, which also helps explain ISKCON's expansion and decline. At ISKCON's inception, Prabhupada was the main resource for ISKCON. Through his teaching of the principles of Krishna consciousness coupled with his charismatic authority, he was able to attract youths willing to participate in his mission. When he arrived in the United States in 1965, his material resources consisted of a suitcase, an umbrella, a supply of dry cereal, and 200 three-volume sets of his translation of and commentary on the first three cantos of the *Srimad-Bhagavatam* (Satsvarupa das Goswami, 1980a).

As Prabhupada attracted more youths to his mission, ISKCON grew exponentially in the first decade due to its proselytizing efforts. Thus, ISKCON's main resource was human labor in the form of service performed by devotees, the only cost for which was providing the bare necessities of food, shelter, and clothing. This primary resource, in turn, ensured a steady supply of income from donations solicited on the street in exchange for books and other paraphernalia. The flow of cash would ensure the provision of temple buildings, whether rented or owned, and utilities such as electricity and water. As the overhead for maintenance was low, ISKCON was able to amass large sums of capital which were used to purchase temple properties and fund the publication and distribution of Prabhupada's books.

Street proselytization was also a means of recruiting new members (Judah, 1974; Snow, Ekland-Olson, and Zurcher, 1980; Rochford, 1985), who would in turn act as human resources in the service of the mission of ISKCON. In this way, ISKCON's human assets were transformed into physical assets of property and money-producing businesses, the primary one being the BBT, along with smaller businesses including Govinda's vegetarian restaurants and the Spiritual Sky incense business. Specialized labor included large numbers of devotees engaged in publishing Prabhupada's books within the BBT, with devotees skilled in the various aspects of book production, including translating, editing, typesetting, and artwork. However, this large, mostly unpaid, labor force declined as devotees moved out of the ashram due to a decline in book distribution and, with it, the income that had kept ISKCON afloat throughout the 1970s (Rochford, 2007a, p. 63).

Outreach and Proselytization

In its early days in North America and other Western countries, the Hare Krishna movement drew many of its converts from the counterculture and social movement networks. Stark's proposition that new religious movements will succeed to the degree that they can compete with local conventional religions in a relatively unregulated religious economy (Stark, 1996, p. 141) helps explain this phenomenon. Recruitment increased exponentially in the 1970s until expansion slowed in the early 1980s in the period after the death of Prabhupada (Rochford, 2007a) and the anticult initiatives of the 1980s and 1990s. Similarly, in countries where the state more tightly controls the practice of religion – for example, the former Soviet Union – ISKCON's ability to compete has been hampered. Stark has also argued that new religious movements will succeed if they can sustain strong internal attachments, while at the same time remaining an open social network that can form connections to outsiders (Stark, 1996, p. 143). From its initial period, the movement's proselytization efforts depended on being open to newcomers, and this was especially the case from the beginning, by necessity. Early members recall that it was very easy to move into the ashram in the late 1960s and 1970s. This needs to be qualified with the acknowledgment that at that time – and one could say among strict ISKCON devotees today – association with outsiders was considered appropriate for the purpose of recruiting a person to Krishna consciousness, but not for casual social connection. Having joined, members were discouraged from associating with people who were not Krishna devotees, in accordance with the precepts outlined in *The Nectar of Devotion* (Prabhupada, 2012, p. 69).

Preaching in the 1960s involved inviting people in the counterculture scene to Prabhupada's lectures through word of mouth. Proselytization methods then took on a more targeted focus beginning with the first public performance of *harinam sankirtan* (congregational chanting) in Tompkins Square Park, New York City, in October 1966 (Satsvarupa das Goswami, 1980a). In the 1970s and 1980s, outreach methods consisted mostly of distributing Prabhupada's books and magazines on the street, in shopping malls, and in airports in exchange for donations, which were a mainstay of ISKCON's fundraising efforts. By 1980, book distribution had fallen dramatically and was replaced largely with selling record albums, candles, and food (Rochford, 2007a, pp. 62–3), as well as stickers and paintings in a practice that devotees colloquially called "the pick." Public venues for these activities included streets in busy commercial and retail areas, airports, and, later on, music festivals. Although book distribution has continued as a form of proselytization, and can be perceived as rather direct by members of the public, the aggressive approach of the 1970s and 1980s has been toned down.

The 1990s saw yet more innovations including softer, more indirect methods than the "in your face" book distribution methods of the 1970s and 1980s that had at times annoyed the public, local authorities, and businesses. In the 1990s, the amalgamation of American straightedge punk and the Hare Krishna movement resulted in the "Krishnacore" music scene that attracted youths to the movement (Dines, 2015, p. 147). By the early 2000s, devotees were a fixture at music festivals, Burning Man and the Rainbow Gathering in the United States, Glastonbury in the United Kingdom, Woodstock Festival Poland (now called Pol'and'Rock Festival), and the Mind Body Spirit Festival held in cities around the world. Holding *kirtan* and teaching yoga at yoga studios and retreats started to become popular. Teaching vegetarian and vegan cooking and opening vegetarian restaurants continued the trend of a softer approach to outreach (see Figure 11). Temples became less of a focus of proselytization and more of a place of worship for Indian-Hindu immigrants, so those involved in outreach found other places to

Figure 11 Govinda's vegetarian restaurant at the ISKCON London Radha-Krishna Temple, London, United Kingdom, September 10, 2009. Photo by Ilya Mauter. Wikimedia Commons.

cultivate new recruits. In effect, the Hinduization and Indianization of many of ISKCON's temples, particularly in the United States, United Kingdom, and Australia, has meant that preaching has moved to other spheres. This has involved more emphasis on Hare Krishna restaurants, *kirtan* at yoga studios, and an increase in *kirtan*, book, and *prasadam* distribution at festivals.

Several farm communities have pivoted to ecovillages and retreat centers. While this is faithful to Prabhupada's espoused principle of "simple living and high thinking," it nevertheless involves an adjustment in identity to align with prevailing trends in broader society that focus on addressing climate change and sustainable living. The ISKCON website lists eighty-eight rural communities globally. Of those, four rural communities located in West Virginia, Brazil, the Phillipines, and Maharasthra in India are officially called ecovillages (ISKCON, 2016a). In his studies of ISKCON ecovillages in Scotland, England, and Hungary, Lestar (2018) positions Hare Krishna as an environmental movement, rather than focusing on its religious aspect. Farkas (2021) notes the increased emic interpretation of the Krishna Valley farm community in Hungary as an ecovillage, in line with the rise of the Hungarian ecovillage movement. By contrast, the ecovillage in Maharasthra has been conceptualized as such from its inception (ISKCON, 2016a). Govinda Valley on the outskirts of Sydney, Australia was purchased with the intention of running a retreat center and identifies itself as a yogic community, hosting spiritual and yoga retreats (Govinda Valley, no date). In a surprising juxtaposition, New Vrindaban in West Virginia boasts organic gardens, a cow sanctuary, a yoga studio, and scenic hikes (New Vrindaban, 2021b) alongside land leased out by New Vrindaban for fracking natural gas (Rose, 2020).

Branding *Bhakti*

Karapanagiotis (2021) has noted that innovative marketing strategies that aim to successfully pitch Krishna consciousness to Westerners are a growing trend in ISKCON. She has coined this strategy "the branding of *bhakti*" and those behind these efforts as "Krishna branders" – ISKCON members who are "rebranding the ISKCON movement as mindfulness, yoga, and meditation in order to attract more [W]esterners" (Karapanagiotis, 2021, p. 15). Karapanagiotis identifies three new ISKCON brands, each led by an ISKCON guru, that are radically different outreach spaces from the traditional ISKCON temple. Devamrita Swami and his disciples have been setting up preaching spaces designed to cater to Westerners that consist of urban meditation lofts and mantra lounges with the branding of an "edgy meditation and mindfulness-based social club" (Karapanagiotis, 2021, p. 16). A preaching initiative led by

Radhanath Swami brands ISKCON as the theological heart of postural yoga, the essence of which is devotion to Krishna. The objective is to assist participants to transition from yoga to Krishna consciousness. Radhanath Swami and his disciples have established ISKCON temples inside yoga studios and yoga retreat centers in the United States and India where they host events, retreats, and yoga teacher training programs led by Western yoga teachers. Finally, Krishna West, the brainchild of Hridayananda das Goswami, aims to attract Westerners by presenting Krishna consciousness stripped of Indian culture, which he sees as an impediment to making it appealing and relevant to them. This involves Westernizing clothing, food, and musical instruments (Karapanagiotis, 2021, p. 17). The first two brands' attempts to innovate and rebrand Krishna consciousness align with Snow, Ekland-Olson, and Zurcher (1980, p. 472), who argue that a social movement may embrace interests or points of view that are secondary to its main purpose, but are important to potential members. By doing so, the movement aims to increase its membership by aligning with the values or interests of potential members.

While Karapanagiotis' research suggests that a divide is being created between traditional ISKCON temples and new preaching spaces dedicated to drawing in Westerners, taking this view would oversimplify what is occurring throughout ISKCON, based on research carried out in the United States and parts of India. Some of the conclusions about the Hinduization of ISKCON do not apply to all parts of the organization. Similarly, the Krishna branding phenomenon applies to some but not all geographic locations of ISKCON. It is not the case that all ISKCON temples have become predominantly Indian-Hindu congregations and bastions of Hindu culture. If we look at ISKCON globally, including Europe, we see that there are several temples which do not have a large proportion of the membership from an Indian-Hindu background. Russia, Ukraine, Latvia, and Estonia, for example, have a high proportion of devotees from local and non-Indian backgrounds. In other cases, ISKCON temples themselves are transforming to meet the needs of Westerners. A temple in the Belgian countryside, for example, hosts busloads of tourists every year, holds yoga retreats, and has comfortable accommodations, a restaurant, and a bakery to meet the tastes and needs of visitors (Radhadesh, no date).

Educational Communities for Adults and Children

In line with the Gaudiya Vaishnava tradition of passing on knowledge through a line of teachers, ISKCON has several educational and academic projects and affiliates. These are internally focused educational programs designed to educate devotees and their children, both as a part of helping them to advance spiritually and to keep them within the fold. Other projects serve as a form of proselytization to bring in new members. Foremost among these educational projects is ISKCON's publishing arm, BBT, which publishes all of Prabhupada's translations and commentaries on Vaishnava texts and transcriptions of his lectures and conversations. Publication of these books is a key part of proselytization, as books are distributed to the public as well as devotees. Although book distribution is much reduced from its peak in the1970s and early 1980s, it remains a core proselytization practice. The Bhaktivedanta Vedabase is an online database of all Prabhupada's published work, letters, and transcribed talks (Bhaktivedanta Book Trust International, Inc., no date).

Established in 1987 as an educational institute in Vrindavan in accordance with the wishes of Prabhupada, the VIHE is intended as a way for devotees to improve their *sadhana*, develop devotional qualities, engage in the study of Vaishnava scriptural texts, associate with senior devotees, and receive training in management and preaching skills (VIHE, 2019). The Bhaktivedanta Institute (BI) was set up by Dr. T. D. Singh (Svarupa Damodara Goswami) in 1974 at the direction of Prabhupada. Its purpose is to deliberate upon the core values and bigger questions of life and the cosmos through the interface of modern science with spiritual traditions. The institute organizes conferences, seminars, and lectures and publishes academic research (Bhaktivedanta Institute, 2021). Other educational projects that constitute academic communities within the Hare Krishna movement include the ISKCON Studies Institute, Bhaktivedanta College in Belgium, the Alfred Ford School of Management, and the Institute for Vaishnava Studies. These initiatives are in different stages of development and have had varying degrees of success; nevertheless, they collectively contribute to the academic community within the movement. Publications include *Back to Godhead, ISKCON Communications Journal* and *Journal of Vaishnava Studies*, the latter being academic journals.

Stark proposes that to succeed, religious movements need to socialize their young members sufficiently well to minimize both defection and the appeal of reduced strictness (Stark, 1996, p. 144). Prabhupada seemed to understand this need because in the 1970s he oversaw the establishment of *gurukulas* in ISKCON. In the Vedic tradition, a *gurukula* literally means "the house of the guru" and it is where young people receive an education that corresponds to the tradition's precepts (Bryant and Ekstrand, 2004, p. 444). Prabhupada expected all devotees to send their children to *gurukulas* and in many cases this involved sending children to either boarding schools or day schools. However, when endemic child abuse at the *gurukulas* was revealed, the reputation of the schools was damaged. For this reason, many ISKCON members now send their children to secular schools. Nonetheless, ISKCON still has several schools for educating children, some called *gurukulas* and others simply called schools, possibly to distance themselves from a brand that has negative connotations attached to it.

There are ISKCON-affiliated *gurukulas* in North America, South America, India, Africa, and Australia (ISKCON, 2016b), indicating the importance for many devotees of having a spiritually based education for their children. For example, Goloka Community School was established in 2018 in Hillsborough, North Carolina and has attracted many new students, including some whose families moved to Hillsborough specifically to enroll their children at the school. It was started as a homeschool co-op and is working on attaining private school status. The teaching is Montessori-style, adding Krishna-conscious elements to the curriculum. The head teacher argues that ISKCON needs to focus on improving childcare and education: "So many gurukulis [graduates of *gurukulas*] have grown and are grihasthas [married householders] now with their own kids. We're ready for gurukulas, and we're ready for ones that last; that are safe; professionally run" (Smullen, 2019, para. 24).

Virtual Communities

In the twenty-first century, connecting online has become an important way in which members of the Hare Krishna movement can associate with each other. Online communities have served to fill gaps for devotees who are geographically distant from ISKCON communities or estranged from ISKCON as an institution but who still desire involvement with devotees and Krishna-conscious philosophy. The online presence takes the form of several official ISKCON forums including Krishna.com, Dandavats.com, and ISKCON.org. Individuals connect with others as friends and followers on social media platforms, most notably Facebook, as well as Twitter and Instagram. Various Facebook groups and pages for ISKCON centers and communities, and disciple groups for members with the same guru, serve as points of contact. Other pages are dedicated to specific interests, such as theological and philosophical discourse, vegetarian and vegan cooking, *kirtan* groups, festivals, and cow protection. However, along with providing a way for devotees to connect, online forums have also served as an arena in which disagreements and disputes have played out. In this space, the movement's most sensitive issues are often laid bare, hashed out in protracted discussions that can last for weeks, months, or years. Disputes and disagreements within the movement predate the Internet and social media, but the online space has served to exacerbate existing disputes and helped to seed new ones due to the fast-flowing nature and wide reach of virtual communications.

Responses to the COVID-19 Pandemic

The COVID-19 pandemic has had significant effects on how Hare Krishna devotees come together as a community. As governments around the world mandated social distancing and prohibited large gatherings throughout the pandemic, in-person visits to temples were reduced. Some temple ashram residents became sick with COVID-19 and had to quarantine in the ashram or go to hospital, forcing temples to cut back their services and temporarily close their doors to visitors. As temple attendance dropped, online streaming of temple services filled the gap (Kalyana Giriraj Das, 2022). Many festivals, an important part of the tradition's way of commemorating holy days, moved online. Online communities also served to fill the gap left by in-person association between devotees.

Zeller (2021) analyzes ISKCON's approach to dealing with the pandemic in terms of frame alignment. He notes that in the early days of the pandemic, in March 2020, ISKCON Mayapura – considered a global headquarters within ISKCON – aligned with Indian public health measures and mainstream scientific approaches to fighting the spread of COVID-19. These measures included social distancing protocols restricting visitors to the temple and following lockdown mandates. In effect, ISKCON's leaders and members in India followed the local authorities by treating COVID-19 as a public health problem. Other ISKCON communities followed ISKCON Mayapura's example, with centers in Belgium, Sweden, Germany, Australia, the United States, and Canada adopting the local health requirements set by authorities in their geographical locations (see Figure 12). In doing this, Zeller argues, ISKCON's leaders

Figure 12 A devotee wears a protective mask while offering respects to a *murti* of Prabhupada during the COVID-19 pandemic, Rio de Janeiro, Brazil, August 3, 2020. Photo by Andre Coelho/Stringer. Getty Images.

aligned with the frame of trust in scientific authorities, public health measures, and collective action for the common good. Zeller notes that ISKCON had already shifted its frame alignment in the preceding decades, when its leaders and members worked to align their values with mainstream society.

This unified and public response has not been uniform throughout the movement, however. Posts on social media platforms such as Facebook are replete with comments by devotees who subscribe to conspiracy theories about the pandemic, including doubts that COVID-19 is real (in conspiracy theory emic language it is a "plandemic"), and are hesitant about or resistant to taking the COVID-19 vaccine. Debates on personal and group pages on Facebook have raged between those who wish to follow public health advice, including being vaccinated, and those who resist lockdowns, social distancing, and taking the vaccine.

Conclusion

While institutional and community structures and dynamics at play in the Hare Krishna movement have been presented, this is by no means an exhaustive account of the complex set of dynamics that is the Hare Krishna movement. However, the main historical trends in institutional and community dynamics in the movement's history have been highlighted. Frame alignment, resource mobilization theory, and Stark's theoretical system have been used to analyze the Hare Krishna movement's institutional dynamics. Frame alignment shows how ISKCON's relationship with broader society shifted from the 1960s, when its frames aligned with those of the counterculture to become aligned with the Indian-Hindu community. The movement's frames shifted again to align with trends in broader society, including responses to climate change, efforts toward sustainability, and increased interest in yoga, meditation, and veganism. Resource mobilization theory helps to explain how the Hare Krishna movement expanded from its modest beginnings. It also explains how and why it changed from a movement of Westerners living a monastic lifestyle to a congregation-based movement increasingly inhabited by followers from Indian-Hindu backgrounds. Stark's framework similarly illuminates how and why the movement changed in its attitude to and relationship with wider society.

The distinction between ISKCON as a hard institutional structure and the broader Hare Krishna movement has been discussed with the underlying premise that a movement extends beyond any corporate structure devised to give the founder's mission longevity. O'Connell's conceptualization of hard, medium, and soft institutions is essential in making a distinction between ISKCON as an institution and the broader Hare Krishna movement. This understanding provides clarity when grappling with the nuances of the movement and takes account of the varying types of participation that combine to form it. Recent sociopolitical events, including the rise of social media, climate change, and the COVID-19 pandemic, have altered the landscape within which the movement is placed and to which it responds, forcing it to pivot yet again. Navigating this complexity has laid the groundwork for getting a sense of the key challenges that the movement's followers have faced.

4 Issues, Controversies, and Challenges

This section addresses the key challenges and controversies that have character-ized the Hare Krishna movement since its inception. As there have been many such issues, only the most significant ones will be examined. During the 1970s and 1980s, disputes with wider society persisted, including ethically questionable street proselytization practices, charges of brainwashing, confrontational relation-ships with state authorities, and legal disputes with private individuals and public entities. The issue of succession and child abuse in ISKCON's schools proved to be among the most serious challenges that ISKCON as an institution would have to grapple with. Doctrinal disagreements, charges of heresy, and editing changes to Prabhupada's published translations of Vaishnava scriptural texts became controversial topics. The treatment of women has been a point of contention since the 1970s and the controversy regarding female gurus is ongoing. The legitimacy of new preaching initiatives has also been called into question in a series of heated debates. More recently, conspiracy theories and divisions between Russian and Ukrainian devotees in the wake of the Russian invasion of Ukraine have proven to be new causes for concern within the movement.

Disputes with Wider Society

Stark (1996) emphasizes the importance of cultural continuity of a new religious movement with its host culture. Although the Hare Krishna movement was aligned in many ways with the subculture of the counterculture, many of the early chal-lenges it faced were characterized by disputes with wider society due to a lack of cultural continuity and frame alignment with its host cultures. These quarrels with wider society took up much of the attention of the movement's leaders and the news media. The following subsections discuss the most prominent external disputes.

Charges of Brainwashing and Mind Control

In the mid-1970s ISKCON in the United States came under attack from depro-grammers and other opponents of cults (Rochford, 2007a, p. 13). Charges of brainwashing and mind control were leveled against ISKCON, which was char-acterized as a dangerous cult. In a landmark case, charges of brainwashing and mind control were brought against the New York temple on behalf of the parents of Ed Shapiro and Marylee Kreshower. The judge dismissed the case in 1977, stating that Hare Krishna is a bona fide religion with roots in India. This was the first case of brainwashing against a contemporary new religious movement and the first of many legal cases brought against ISKCON (Shinn, 1987, pp. 122–3). The most notorious legal case was that of Robin George, a fifteen-year-old girl who ran away from home to join the Laguna Beach temple and was subsequently moved by devotees between various ISKCON temples in order to evade her parents (Court of Appeal, Fourth District, Division 1, California, 1992). Robin George later left the movement of her own accord and, with her mother, brought a lawsuit against ISKCON that included charges of false imprisonment, infliction of emotional distress, libel, and the wrongful death of Robin George's father, who died of a heart attack soon after her return home. The charges rested on claims of brainwashing and mind control. The lawsuit threatened to bankrupt ISKCON in North America when Robin George and her mother were awarded $32.5 million, which was later reduced to $9.6 million (Shinn, 1987, pp. 123, 168).

Brainwashing claims were not confined to the United States. In Hungary, a Reformed Church minister launched an attack against the movement in many newspapers in 1991, arguing that devotees were brainwashed, split from their families, had lost consciousness of being Hungarian, and were treated like slaves. He alleged that the movement was inflicting psychological terror, utilized aggressive psycho-technology, exercised total control and cunningness, and perverted individual personality. He subsequently founded an anticult movement followed by an attempt to have ISKCON, as well as three other religions, branded as "destructive sects" and to have government support removed from them. (Hungary, like many European nations, has state-supported religion.) This attempt was soon after withdrawn by the Hungarian parliament, which recognized ISKCON's religious life and charitable work (Kamarás, 1999).

In the 1990s, Introvigne (1997) argued that the claim that a religious group does not have voluntary membership was a rhetorical tool used to discredit that group. The same tool was applied to distinguish between religions joined voluntarily and cults joined due to brainwashing – later identified by the euphemisms mind control, mental manipulation or mental destabilization, as the brainwashing theory was discredited by mental health scholars. In 1987, the Board of Social and Ethical Responsibility for Psychology of the American Psychological Association concluded that the mind control theories used to distinguish cults from religions are not part of accepted psychological science (Introvigne, 1997).

State-Sponsored Persecution and
Violence in the Former Soviet Union and Russia

While charges of brainwashing and mind control were being leveled against ISKCON in the United States during the 1980s, devotees were experiencing persecution in the Soviet Union. The International Society for Krishna Consciousness was established in the Soviet Union in 1971 when Prabhupada visited Moscow and initiated his first disciple, Anatoli Pinyayev (Anderson, 1986, p. 316), and gave him the name Ananta Shanti das. Ananta Shanti's proselytization efforts established the movement in the Soviet Union – Prabhupada's visit in 1971 was to be his only trip there. In 1980, two ISKCON leaders visited Russia and attempted to organize a *kirtan* and a lecture in Riga. However, devotees were dispersed by the police and KGB agents, the two foreign guests were advised to leave the country (Petrova, 2013, p. 112) and attendees were interrogated (Anderson, 1986, p. 316). A KGB agent stated that "the three greatest threats to the Soviet Union were Western Culture, pop music and Hare Krishna" (Petrova, 2013, p. 112).

Beginning in 1981, devotees attempted to form legal religious associations, and were told that the KGB would continue to break up their meetings until they did so. However, their applications were refused due to being "ideologically deviant" and the organizers were later arrested and sentenced to labor camps. From 1982, the movement attracted negative press coverage, including claims that it was funded by the CIA with the objective of undermining the spiritual unity of the Soviet people. The first arrest occurred in 1981, when a devotee was sentenced to one year in camp on charges of "parasitism." In 1984, police raided the homes of devotees in the Stavropol region and nine were sentenced to labor camp terms of one to five years. In 1985, police raided meetings of devotees on a regular basis, warning attendees that they were illegal; after devotees made attempts to register ISKCON, their homes were searched and they were interrogated. Four devotees were later arrested, and another was diagnosed as suffering from "Krishna mania" and committed to a psychiatric hospital (Anderson, 1986, pp. 316–17). In the early and mid-1980s, several dozen Hare Krishna followers were incarcerated in prisons, psychiatric hospitals, and labor camps because of their practice of Krishna consciousness (Jakupko, 1986). While detained they were beaten, tortured, force fed with non-vegetarian foods, subjected to psychiatric abuse, forced to perform hard labor, and subjected to other human rights violations. Some devotees in mental hospitals died from large doses of antipsychotic medication and insulin (Petrova, 2013, p. 113).

Devotees and their families wrote to leaders including President Mikhail Gorbachev, President Ronald Reagan, President Rajiv Gandhi, and Pope John Paul II. From the late 1980s and the 1990s, when the liberalization of religion began, the situation gradually began to change, and devotees were slowly released from incarceration. Religious freedom in Russia after perestroika and the passing of the liberal law "On Freedom of Consciousness" in 1990 was brief, and followed by concerns that cults posed a threat to society and the state. Objections to nonmainstream religions came from the Russian Orthodox Church as well as the anticult movement, which was represented by Orthodox priests and laypersons (Petrova, 2013, pp. 113–14).

In Soviet era Lithuania, ISKCON developed as an underground movement under the threat of KGB repressions. The practice of Krishna consciousness there was a form of resistance to the Soviet regime and its communist ideology, and ISKCON in Lithuania was instrumental in the expansion of ISKCON in the Soviet Union. After the imprisonment of Hare Krishna devotees who had been printing Prabhupada's books in Armenia, devotees in Lithuania took over the secret printing and distribution of ISKCON literature throughout the Soviet region (Pranskevičiūtė and Juras, 2014, p. 16). *Salted Bread* is a personal memoir that chronicles the story of two childhood friends who joined the Hare Krishna movement in Armenia in the 1980s, after which they were initiated as Sachisuta das and Sarvabhavana das. In 1986, they were arrested by the KGB and incarcerated in a labor camp until 1987, when Sachisuta das died just eleven days before his scheduled release (Buniatyan and Buniatyan, 2007).

Hare Krishna devotees in Armenia were violently attacked three times in six months from 1994 to 1995 (ISKCON Communications Europe, 1994; ISKCON Communications Journal, 1995). The attack in 1995 appeared to be perpetrated by a paramilitary group armed with automatic weapons, submachine guns, other guns, metal rods, and metal chains. The group destroyed the temple in Yerevan and severely beat devotees, leaving twelve requiring hospital treatment and forcing devotees to go into hiding. Armenian police ignored complaints, although one policeman commented that the attack occurred because the devotees were deviating from the national tradition. Shortly after the attack, a man walked into the Yerevan temple and claimed that it had happened because the devotees were not following the religion of the national church (Back To Godhead, 1995; ISKCON Communications Journal, 1995).

In 2011, prosecutors in the Siberian city of Tomsk filed a legal case to have Prabhupada's translation and commentary of the *Bhagavad Gita* ruled as extremist material and placed on a list of banned publications. Hare Krishna devotees in Russia saw the case as an effort by the Russian Orthodox Church to restrict their activities. The case was dismissed by a Russian court in 2011 (BBC News, 2011). The ISKCON temple in Moscow was demolished by the government in 2004 to make way for an apartment complex and replacement land was granted, only to then be taken away (ISKCON News, 2013). Permits to build a new temple were granted but then withdrawn a number of times (Eremenko, 2014). In 2021, the

European Court of Human Rights (ECHR) ruled that Russian policies against cults violated the European principle of freedom of religion or belief. One of the cases involved several instances of discrimination against ISKCON, including statements made by a Russian Orthodox priest that the organization was a "demonically oriented religion," which "profoundly affected the personality" of its followers (Introvigne, 2021). A taxpayer-funded local government brochure titled *Watch Out for Cults!* called ISKCON, together with other movements, a "totalitarian cult" and a "destructive cult" (Introvigne, 2021). Stark proposes that "new religious movements will prosper to the extent that they compete against weak, local conventional religious organizations within a relatively unregulated religious economy" (Stark, 1996, p. 141). During the 1980s and 1990s, ISKCON was clearly perceived by Soviet authorities to be competing with Russia's conventional Orthodox Christian Church. This concern continues to be an issue today, albeit one with less severe consequences for devotees than during the days of the Soviet Union.

Legal Disputes

In addition to the brainwashing cases noted, and the child abuse lawsuit (discussed in the subsection "Child Abuse in the *Gurukulas*"), ISKCON's fraught relationships with wider society are evidenced by other legal disputes. In the mid-1970s, airports, state fairs, and other public venues in the United States began to legally challenge ISKCON's book distribution practices, arguing that its tactics were more financial than religious and thereby not protected by First Amendment privileges. Compounding the situation was the reality that book distribution practices were sometimes deceptive and unethical. The courts began restricting ISKCON's use of public spaces, including setting time limits and curtailing the number of devotees who could distribute books at any given time. In the late 1970s, some states won cases to abridge devotees' access to fair patrons. Beginning in 1977 and 1978, cases were heard that sought to prevent book distribution in all public places, including airports in Los Angeles, Seattle, and Chicago, with the Chicago airport being closed to book distribution in 1978. In 1981, a US Supreme Court ruling prevented ISKCON from distributing books at fairs across the country (Rochford, 1985, pp. 186–7). The legal restriction of book distribution, a key form of fundraising, had a significant impact on ISKCON's financial well-being.

The fight to prevent the closure of Bhaktivedanta Manor in the United Kingdom garnered a great deal of public attention, both because it dragged on for years and because the Indian-Hindu community was mobilized in the effort. The disagreement arose because, as increasing numbers of Hindus visited the temple, the small village in which it was situated became clogged with long lines of traffic and parked cars, particularly on Sundays and festival days. Village residents made complaints to the local council that ISKCON did not have planning permission for large-scale worship; they only had permission for a theological college for the promotion of Krishna consciousness. The complaints evolved into a series of legal disputes with the local council and the national government in the 1980s and 1990s. Believing that its religious freedom had been violated, ISKCON took its claim to the courts, including the ECHR. Although ISKCON had experienced a number of legal defeats, in 1996 the organization was given planning permission to operate as a place of worship. This decision was made after it agreed to construct a new access driveway through the newly purchased adjoining property, thereby preventing visitor traffic from going through the village (Nye, 2001). The success of the campaign to save Bhaktivedanta Manor hinged upon successfully mobilizing the Hindu community to support the legal case and public relations campaign by engaging in volunteer activities and peaceful protest.

Internal Disputes

While internal disagreements have beset the movement from its earliest days, clashes with wider society took up much of the attention of the movement's leaders in the 1970s and 1980s. As tension with wider society reduced, the movement's controversies increasingly became internal ones; due to their prevalence, only the most significant disputes are discussed in this section.

The Issue of Succession

The first major internal setback came with the death of the founder in 1977 – an event that sent shockwaves through the movement. In the months leading up to Prabhupada's death, the issue of succession became increasingly foregrounded and, after his death, eleven of his most prominent disciples became the spiritual heads of the movement. The assumption of these roles was not without controversy, and was at the core of questions about what form leadership would take in the following decades. A series of internal quarrels ensued, including questions of authority surrounding the role of the guru.

The controversy had its roots in the events of 1977 when Prabhupada's health had started to decline (Satsvarupa das Goswami, 1993d). This situation prompted some members of the GBC to question Prabhupada regarding how the affairs of ISKCON would be managed in his absence (Satsvarupa das Goswami, 1993d, p. 324). In the first of these conversations, in May 1977 (ISKCON Governing Body Commission, 1977), GBC members asked Prabhupada how new members would be initiated after his death. In response, he indicated that he would name some of his disciples to be gurus. This was in accordance with the Vaishnava tradition and scriptures, which state that after the death of the guru the disciple should take on the role of guru and initiate and instruct disciples in spiritual matters. Later that year, in July, when his secretary asked what should be done about the devotees waiting to be initiated, Prabhupada named nine of his male disciples to perform this function on his behalf since he was too sick to do so himself (ISKCON Governing Body Commission, 1977; Satsvarupa das Goswami, 1993d, p. 345; Tamal Krishna Goswami, 1999, pp. 111–12). The disciples were: Kirtanananda Swami, Satsvarupa das Goswami, Jayatirtha das, Bhagavan das, Harikesa Swami, Jayapataka Swami, Tamal Krishna Goswami, Ramesvara Swami, and Hridayananda das Goswami (Prabhupada and Tamal Krishna Goswami, 1977). Bhavananda Goswami and Hansadutta Swami were added to the list by Tamal Krishna Goswami soon after the conversation, bringing the total number of men initiating on Prabhupada's behalf to eleven (Burt, 2013, p. 112).

On November 14, 1977, Prabhupada passed away in India at the age of eighty-one. A few months later, at the annual GBC meeting in Mayapura in March 1978, the issue of succession arose when the matter of how the leadership of ISKCON would continue became the main point of discussion. In his will, Prabhupada had named the GBC as the ultimate managing authority (Satsvarupa das Goswami, 1993d, p. 326). What needed to be clarified was who would be the spiritual authority in ISKCON now that Prabhupada was no longer present. At the GBC meeting in March 1978 the governing body resolved that, "A GBC committee will be formed consisting of GBC members who are initiating Gurus. They will choose new gurus once per year in Mayapur" (ISKCON Governing Body Commission, 1978). The eleven disciples who had already been acting in senior management roles and initiating disciples on Prabhupada's behalf, most of whom were GBC members, immediately took on the role of guru. Within the movement there was a perception that they had effectively become the successors to Prabhupada. However, some other GBC members claimed that there was no decision made by the GBC as a body that the eleven men would become gurus, and that it was not discussed at the GBC meeting. They asserted that the decision was made among the eleven who became gurus (Burt, 2013, pp. 114–16).

Nevertheless, the eleven gurus were accepted by most ISKCON members, although a few expressed their discontent. In the early 1980s, rumblings of opposition persisted in the form of discussions and mimeographed papers that were circulated among leaders. The chorus of opposition grew louder as some of the gurus started to have difficulties and leader malfeasance became a problem within their ranks. Some gurus had difficulty in maintaining their vows of celibacy and abstention from intoxication, in some cases having sexual relations with disciples or other devotees. Some engaged in illegal activities, including Hansadutta who was stockpiling weapons at one of the ISKCON properties under his jurisdiction. In response, the GBC removed him from his positions of guru and GBC member and expelled him from ISKCON in 1983. Kirtanananda was alleged to be engaged in pedophilia, racketeering, and presiding over the murders of devotees critical of his leadership; he was later convicted of some of the alleged crimes. Another guru, Jayatirtha, had been taking LSD and engaging in sexual relationships with female disciples before leaving ISKCON in 1982 with some of his disciples; a disgruntled disciple brutally murdered him in 1987.

This situation led to increasing levels of alarm within the institution of ISKCON and coalesced into a guru reform movement that brought about sweeping changes in the position of the guru. The most significant change was the removal of the zonal arrangement that required uninitiated devotees to take initiation and instruction from the guru in their zone, in what became known as the "zonal *acharya* system."[18] This development meant that devotees would be able to take initiation from a guru of their own choosing. In addition, the lavish ritualistic worship bestowed upon the zonal gurus was eliminated and replaced with a more moderate approach. Finally, Prabhupada was reaffirmed as the topmost human spiritual authority in ISKCON. By the time the reforms were enacted, only five of the eleven gurus remained in their positions (Burt, 2019). In 1986, Bhavananda was removed from his position of guru due to revelations that he had broken his vows, and Ramesvara and Bhagavan left their positions due to difficulties in following the requirements of being a renunciate (Burt, 2013). Although the issue of succession was resolved on a bureaucratic level in 1987, it is still considered to be one of the most controversial issues within ISKCON.

Stark proposes that religious movements succeed to the degree that they have legitimate leaders with adequate authority to be effective. Authority, in turn, requires doctrinal justifications and it is regarded as legitimate and is effective if members perceive themselves as participants in the system of authority (Stark, 1996, p. 139). During the crisis of succession, when some of ISKCON's members opposed the positions that the zonal *acharyas* had taken, a great deal of ink was spilled in discussions that made reference to Gaudiya Vaishnava texts as well as Prabhupada's writings, lectures, and conversations. The debate centered on whether the eleven gurus were following the Gaudiya Vaishnava tradition. With respect to Stark's second point, some of Prabhupada's

---

[18] *Acharya* is another name for a guru. In ISKCON, it took on the meaning of a successor to Prabhupada as the religious head of the institution.

male disciples considered that they had been excluded from decision-making, with the role of ultimate spiritual authority within the institution being usurped by their godbrothers.

One result of ISKCON's crisis of succession and the resulting loss of faith in its gurus was the appearance of a doctrine called the *ritvik acharya* theory. Adherents of this position claim that Prabhupada appointed *ritviks* (priests) as proxies to initiate devotees on his behalf and did not intend for his disciples to become gurus in their own right. Foundational to this position is the belief that Prabhupada is the only legitimate guru for devotees within ISKCON (Tamal Krishna Goswami, 1997). This is at odds with Prabhupada's statement in 1977 that his disciples should initiate their own disciples after this death (ISKCON Governing Body Commission, 1977) and, in doing so, continue the tradition of *parampara* or disciplic succession by which the Gaudiya Vaishnava tradition is perpetuated. *The Final Order* is the most well-known publication that outlines the *ritvik* position (Desai, 1996). The *ritvik* position has a pervasive presence online and continues to attract support from a number of devotees. Some devotees have officially left ISKCON because of their adherence to the position and the GBC's rejection of it as heresy. The persistence of the *ritvik* position signifies that for some ISKCON devotees the guru reforms did not completely resolve the guru issue (Burt, 2013).

Child Abuse in the Gurukulas

The addition of children to ISKCON's community came after members married and produced progeny. In 1968, Prabhupada began planning to establish *guruku-las* – ashram-based boarding schools – to train students in spiritual life. There was an expectation from ISKCON's leadership that all parents would send their children to the *gurukula* to be raised by ISKCON's teachers. Parents largely accepted theological and other justifications offered by the leadership for remaining uninvolved in the lives of their children and sacrificing parental authority for the benefit of children's self-realization. Another purpose of the *gurukula* was to free parents from child-rearing so they could commit all their energy to the needs of the movement in various kinds of service (Rochford, 2007a, p. 60). To that end, many children were removed from the care of their parents at the age of four or five and sent to the *gurukula* (Rochford, 2007a, p. 59).

Gurukulas were established globally, most prominently in the United States and India, but also in Western Europe, South Africa, and Australia. In the *gurukulas*, a significant number of children were physically, psychologically, and sexually abused by teachers and older children acting on a teacher's behalf. Yet reports to ISKCON's leadership by concerned parents, teachers, and students often fell on deaf ears or, if taken seriously, were covered up (Rochford and Heinlein, 1998). Rochford's 1998 youth survey of 115 former *gurukula* students aged fifteen to thirty-four found that 25 percent had been sexually abused for more than one year, and 29 percent had experienced sexual abuse for a period of between one month and one year. Thirty-one percent indicated that they had been physically abused (Rochford, 2007a, p. 75). All but two ashram-based *gurukulas* were closed down and replaced with community day schools and many children were sent to mainstream public schools (Rochford and Heinlein, 1998). At a meeting of North American ISKCON leaders in 1996, former *gurukula* students related the abuse they had suffered. In response, the GBC established a "Task Force on Child Abuse in ISKCON" in 1997. The ISKCON Central Office of Child Protection (ICOCP) was established based on the recommendations of the Task Force. In March 1998, the ICOCP was incorporated as the Association for the Protection of Vaishnava Children.[19] Children of Krishna, Inc. was established by *gurukula* alumni as an independent, grassroots organization dedicated to helping youth to help themselves (ISKCON Child Protection Office, 2018).

Soon after Rochford (1998) published his article on child abuse, a lawsuit that threatened ISKCON's existence in the United States was filed against it in 2000. The lawsuit alleged that, during the 1970s and 1980s, forty-four former *gurukula* students from the United States, Canada, and the United Kingdom were victims of sexual, emotional, mental, and physical abuse and exploitation in ISKCON's *gurukulas*. The lawsuit sought $400 million in damages. The federal case was dismissed but another lawsuit was filed in a Texas state court in 2001, also seeking $400 million in damages. By 2002, the number of plaintiffs in the case had grown to ninety-two. After several ISKCON communities named in the lawsuit filed for bankruptcy, the case was resolved in 2005 (Rochford, 2007a, pp. 95–6). The case garnered a great deal of attention within ISKCON and in the news media, damaging the organization's reputation when institutionalized child abuse was revealed as one of its darkest secrets.

The Origin of the Soul Controversy

One of the most significant doctrinal disputes within ISKCON has been a controversy about the origin of the soul, known within the movement as "the fall of the *jiva*" controversy.[20] The controversy had its roots in a question

---

[19] The ICOCP has itself been a subject of controversy, with debate within the movement about the approaches that it takes and how much power it has in reporting child abuse and prosecuting alleged perpetrators.

[20] The Sanskrit term *jiva* can be translated into English as "soul."

that arose within ISKCON regarding the paradox of the ontological position of the soul: Did living entities fall from the spiritual realm, where they were enjoying personal relationships with Krishna, into the material existence of repeated birth and death? Or is there no fall from the spiritual realm since souls are described as either eternally liberated or eternally bound in material existence? The seemingly paradoxical nature of Prabhupada's answers to questions on this topic meant that the question lingered. Other Gaudiya Vaishnava groups and gurus outside of ISKCON had a different interpretation of how souls that are meant to be eternally liberated come to be in the material world, adding to the confusion. As new translations of important Vaishnava texts were published and the translations differed from Prabhupada's translations and teachings, controversy arose (Tamal Krishna Goswami, 1997).

In 1994, two ISKCON members published a book entitled *In Vaikuntha Not Even the Leaves Fall* (Satyanarayana Dasa and Kundali Dasa, 2019). In the book, the authors argue that based on the writings of Jiva Goswami, one of the *acharyas* in the Gaudiya Vaishnava tradition, the *jiva's* conditioning has no beginning and the living entity cannot fall from Vaikuntha to the material world.[21] This differed from the ISKCON account derived from Prabhupada's translations and commentaries. The issue came to a head in 1995 when the GBC banned the book in ISKCON because they thought this different account of the fall of the *jiva* would disturb the minds of devotees (Satyanarana Dasa and Kundali Dasa, 2019). At the 1995 GBC meeting, the GBC resolved that ISKCON's official stance is the view expressed in Prabhupada's commentary to the *Srimad-Bhagavatam* (4.28.54) – that the original position of the soul is to be in a personal relationship with Krishna, and having rejected that relationship, the soul falls down into the material world (Tamal Krishna Goswami, 1997). Satyanarayana left ISKCON and continued his work by forming the Jiva Institute in Vrindavan (Satyanarayana Dasa and Kundali Dasa, 2019). The following year, the GBC published a book of its own to refute Satyanarayana's arguments entitled *Our Original Position* (ISKCON GBC Press, 1996).

In seeking to understand why a technical detail about the soul matters so much, part of the reason may be found in the fact that the Krishna consciousness is based on the idea that a devotee's main purpose is to return to Krishna in the spiritual world at the end of this life. In short, the goal of liberation, or salvation, is key. Tamal Krishna Goswami (1997) identified two other reasons. First, the authority of Prabhupada's translations and teachings seemed to be in competition with the translations and teachings of other Gaudiya Vaishnava groups. Second, since the Gaudiya Vaishnava tradition is a philosophically

---

[21] Vaikuntha is another word for the spiritual world, specifically, the abode of Krishna.

based tradition, the desire of some Gaudiya Vaishnavas to debate theological issues is pervasive.

Prabhupada's Books: Controversial Statements and the Editing Controversy

Additional controversies concern some views expressed by Prabhupada. Members of the Hare Krishna movement have acknowledged that Prabhupada's published works include statements that may be considered offensive to various groups including women, people of various nations and races, members of the LGBTQI community, scholars, scientists, and other Gaudiya Vaishnava groups. Moreover, the works seem to criticize certain ideals of modern Western society including scholarship, science, and democracy. The issue has been discussed by scholars, the GBC, the BBT trustees, and rank and file devotees on online forums. The quandary that devotees loyal to Prabhupada as the founder of the movement find themselves in is the desire to preserve Prabhupada's teachings, while acknowledging the detrimental effect such statements can have on potential converts and devotees from some groups. This is especially important considering that Prabhupada's books have been key to ISKCON's proselytizing efforts and reading them is considered a key part of spiritual practice.

In 2008, the BBT addressed the issue by acknowledging that such statements may discourage some from further reading. They considered several solutions, including deleting or revising controversial passages, adding footnotes, adding appendices, publishing free-standing explanatory inserts, and publishing separate books of commentary. They rejected all of these solutions as unsuitable. They decided that the best solution would be a website where readers can go to gain a better understanding of statements from Prabhupada's books that may be controversial because they are contrary to prevailing social norms. The BBT planned to include a brief note on the copyright page of books that would direct readers to the website for guidance on controversial statements (BBT Trustees, 2008). However, my own research has found that no reference to such a website can be found in Prabhupada's books, and an online search failed to locate such a website.

A related issue that has proven to be even more controversial within the movement is the editing of Prabhupada's books. Since 1983, when the BBT published the second edition of Srila Prabhupada's *Bhagavad Gita As It Is*, some devotees have strongly objected to the editing of Prabhupada's books by the BBT. Critics claim that Prabhupada did not give direct approval for such changes and said nothing about the need for further editing. They add that

Prabhupada's original books were fully authorized and approved by Prabhupada and anything later is less authoritative and less authentic. Moreover, many edits are unnecessary and significantly change the meaning of the text. Finally, they assert that to "correct" Prabhupada displays arrogance on the part of the editors (Bhaktivedanta Book Trust, 2012). Because the BBT has provided counterarguments to these claims and has continued to make editorial changes, the debate rages on. A number of online forums exist where arguments against the editing of Prabhupada's books are presented – for example, arsaprayoga.com (Ajit Krishna Dasa, no date) and bookchanges. com (Madhudvisa Dasa, 1998). There are at least two Facebook groups dedicated to this purpose. One is a private Facebook group started in April 2020 by a disciple of Prabhupada who is a textual scholar of the tradition. Over two years after its inception it had 1,569 members. The group is very active, and devotees opposed to the editing of Prabhupada's books hold discussions where they make arguments that support their position. Online debates about editorial changes to Prabhupada's books indicate that the issue remains controversial.

The Marginalization of Women

The position of women in the Hare Krishna movement has been a contentious issue. Scholars noted the disparity between norms in the movement and those of modern Western society in the early 1970s. Judah (1974) observed that the status of women within the Hare Krishna movement would probably not appeal to Americans interested in women's liberation. As evidence, he cited Prabhupada's statements that women have little intelligence, are untrustworthy, should be treated like children, given little freedom, and protected throughout life by their fathers, husbands, and sons. Judah pointed out that this view is in line with ancient Indian law books (Judah, 1974, p. 86). Daner remarked that unmarried women in ISKCON temples in the United States were under the care of ISKCON males and discouraged from leaving the temple on their own, while married women were expected to be submissive and subservient to their husbands. Daner added that American women did not seem to be able to live up to this Vedic ideal (Daner, 1976, p. 68). Women were often expected to stand at the back of the temple room, rarely gave classes in the temple, and were rarely represented in positions of leadership including temple president and GBC member.

Efforts to provide gender equality in ISKCON started in the 1990s. In 1992, ISKCON Communications Europe organized a conference that discussed the issue of women (Lilamayi Gaurangi, 2015). The issue was debated in scholarly articles (Knott, 1995c, 2004; Radha Devi Dasi, 1998; Muster, 2004) and conference presentations (Visakha Dasi, 2000). In 1994, Harikesa Swami, the then GBC representative for Germany, declared that discrimination against women in his GBC zone must stop and he made efforts to ensure the equality of women in temples. In 1996 a female devotee was granted guest status on the GBC and formed the ISKCON Women's Ministry, which held its first conference in 1997.[22] A second female GBC member was added in 1998. A number of women voiced grievances over their treatment in the movement at the GBC meeting in 2000 and the GBC resolved to prioritize the provision of equal facilities, full encouragement, and care and protection of women in ISKCON (Lilamayi Gaurangi, 2015).

Despite these efforts, discrimination against women continued. In 1999 there was an attack on women in ISKCON's temple in Vrindavan during a morning *kirtan*, because women were trying to get to the front of the temple (Muster, 2004, p. 319). Backlash to gender equality efforts occurred in the form of a group called "the GHQ" (the General Headquarters) established in 1998. The group consisted of men and one female, gathered in an email discussion forum where they voiced their concerns about what they perceived as the growing influence of feminism in ISKCON. The group's objectives were to keep women from positions of leadership; to keep them from leading *kirtans* and giving classes; to terminate the Women's Ministry and ban feminist philosophy; and to censor feminist ideas in ISKCON media. As Rochford pointed out, members identified the values of Western society as atheistic, social, political, educational and cultural conventions that were opposed to those of Krishna consciousness (Rochford, 2007a, pp. 140–1). He concluded that growing gender equality signaled to traditionalists that ISKCON was rapidly accommodating to mainstream American society, thus abandoning its goal of building an oppositional religious culture to Western culture, something that they vehemently opposed (Rochford, 2007a, p. 139). In 2008, the GBC Executive Committee denounced the GHQ for belittling and demeaning women with their sexist and misogynist statements. Such writings, they asserted, are not authorized, and are against the principles of ISKCON and Vaishnava culture (ISKCON GBC Executive Committee, 2008).

Since the 1990s, women have taken on leadership roles that were rare in the 1970s and 1980s. They have increasingly taken on temple president roles, although they are still a minority, and there are currently two female GBC members (ISKCON GBC, 2022c). However, gender equality remains an issue within the movement, and the most obvious signifier of this has been the

---

[22] The ISKCON Women's Ministry is now called the ISKCON Vaishnavi Ministry; a Vaishnavi is a female Vaishnava.

absence of female gurus. The question of whether women can become gurus has been a controversial issue. In 2003, the GBC Executive Committee requested ISKCON's Sastric Advisory Council (SAC) to conduct research to determine whether there is *sastric* (scriptural) support for female *diksha* gurus.[23] The request was made because one female devotee's name had been proposed as a candidate to take on the role of guru, for which there were three objections. The SAC concluded that qualified female devotees should be allowed to give initiation in ISKCON and recommended that female candidates should be of minimum age (at least fifty), have been engaged in the practice of Krishna consciousness for twenty-five or thirty years, and have family support (ISKCON GBC, 2022a). In 2009, the GBC resolved that women could initiate disciples in ISKCON provided they met the conditions recommended by the SAC. The GBC specified that a candidate should be at least fifty-five years of age, live under the protection of a male or qualified householder couple or senior Vaishnava or Vaishnavi *sanga*, and receive written permission from the appropriate regional body to give initiation in that region (ISKCON GBC, 2019).

In 2021, the GBC amended its 2019 resolution due to objections by some of the members of the India Bureau, ISKCON India's leadership body (ISKCON News, 2021), who had threatened to leave ISKCON if women were allowed to become gurus (Blumetti, 2019). The amendment was said to be a "culturally sensitive resolution" resulting from a mediation with India Bureau leaders that would allow regional governing bodies in ISKCON, such as the India Bureau, to opt out of the GBC resolution allowing women to become gurus (ISKCON News, 2021). In 2022, the first female in ISKCON fulfilled the requirements to serve as a *diksha* guru (initiating spiritual master). The requirements were clarified by the GBC's 2021 decision, which was reviewed by the Spiritual Advisors Bhagavata Assembly (SABHA), a representative body of global ISKCON devotees that affirmed its support in May 2022. The North American Council of ISKCON confirmed its support for female *diksha* gurus in North America in June 2022. With the green light being given by ISKCON's governing bodies, Narayani devi dasi, a disciple of Prabhupada, became the first female in ISKCON to serve as a *diksha* guru when she formally accepted her first disciple in an initiation ceremony at the ISKCON temple in Alachua, Florida in August 2022 (Kumari Kunti Dasi and Madan Gopal Das, 2022). After many years of discussion and debate regarding the legitimacy of female gurus, this development constitutes a watershed moment in ISKCON's history.

However, shortly thereafter, the India Bureau leaders again voiced their objections to female gurus. Although regions within ISKCON, including

---

[23] A *diksha* guru provides initiation to a disciple.

India, were given the choice to opt out of allowing female gurus, many ISKCON leaders in India did not agree that women should be allowed to initiate in other parts of the world, even those outside of their jurisdiction. They argued that female gurus are not in line with scripture and Vedic culture. The India Bureau requested that the GBC put on hold its resolution authorizing women to be gurus and restart a dialogue with the bureau, adding that it may not be able to control the repercussions that could ensue from the disenfranchisement caused by the resolution. The GBC responded by putting a moratorium on any further initiations by women in ISKCON for up to three years and agreeing to meet with India leaders to try to address their concerns and seek consensus (ISKCON News Staff, 2022b). As a result, the future of female gurus is uncertain due to objections from the India Bureau.

Krishna West

Krishna West, a new preaching innovation started by Hridayananda das Goswami, was established in 2014. Shortly thereafter, Hridayananda scheduled a preaching tour in Europe to promote it. However, due to concern about Krishna West and uncertainty about what it meant for ISKCON, the GBC asked Hridayananda not to travel outside of the United States to Europe or South America. The response to what was perceived by devotees as Hridayananda's ban from Europe led to a flurry of activity on various Internet forums, including Facebook, where followers of Krishna West expressed their outrage and were often met with equally vigorous counterarguments from opponents. A petition requesting the GBC lift the travel ban circulated around the Internet at this time with many devotees signing it (Sharma, 2014). What can best be described as Internet wars regarding Krishna West spiked at this time. Ironically, functioning as a form of free advertising, online debates sparked interest in and knowledge of Krishna West.

From its beginning, Krishna West was, "a movement within a movement," according to Hridayananda. This label undoubtedly caused concern among the GBC, with its suggestion of a separatist mentality that was echoed in many of the discussions that took place on Facebook. Several ISKCON devotees asked whether the Krishna West enterprise was separate from ISKCON. Hridayananda's claim that Krishna West is a "final destination" also caused some consternation, with this phrase being interpreted by some to mean that people attending Krishna West programs would not be encouraged to participate at ISKCON temples. It seems that at least part of the reason for the GBC ban on Hridayananda's preaching tour in Europe was to give it time to work out whether Krishna West was orthodox or heterodox, and what this meant for

ISKCON. Would Krishna West be a competitor? Or a partner? In April 2015, the GBC and Hridayananda issued a joint statement, affirming that Krishna West was indeed part of ISKCON and that Hridayananda was a faithful follower of Prabhupada (ISKCON Governing Body Commission, 2015). With official GBC sanction in hand, Hridayananda das Goswami set off on a tour in the middle of 2015, which included holding preaching programs in Israel, Italy, Spain, France, Germany, Poland, Lithuania, Denmark, Norway, and programs in the USA on the way back to Los Angeles. The tour proved to be successful in terms of spreading Krishna West's following.

Despite Hridayananda's successful tour, not all ISKCON members were happy with the situation. Criticism continued to come from several ISKCON leaders and GBC members, who stated their concern that Krishna West and Hridayananda's presentation of Krishna consciousness deviated from orthodox teachings. In January 2016, two representatives of the GBC met with Hridayananda to discuss Krishna West and Hridayananda's interactions with and comments about the GBC. Clearly, the GBC was not ready to expel Hridayananda from ISKCON and was seeking to find a way to bring about conciliation. Hridayananda had gained a significant following and the threat of the loss of significant numbers of ISKCON devotees in a schism was too great to risk. The GBC and Hridayananda came to an agreement and called a truce in the war of words. The controversy surrounding Krishna West abated and the initiative continues to operate globally within ISKCON.

Other Internal Disputes

Although a number of additional internal debates could be mentioned, the most salient concern attitudes toward the LGBTQI+ community, veganism, conspiracy theories, and the Russo–Ukrainian War. Brief discussions of these issues follow.

Within the Hare Krishna movement, attitudes to the LGBTQI+ community have been controversial due to statements Prabhupada made in his commentaries about homosexuality being "demoniac" (Prabhupada, 1977).[24] In response to negative attitudes toward LGBTI devotees, Amara Das, a disciple of Prabhupada, formed the Gay & Lesbian Vaishnava Association (GALVA) in 2001 as a nonprofit religious online organization offering positive information and support to LGBTI Vaishnavas and Hindus. In 2009 the association established a Facebook page for ongoing discussion (GALVA-108, no date) and, at

---

[24] I am using "LGBTQI+" to reflect current popular usage, including materials published by the United Nations (United Nations, no date), and to acknowledge that conventions vary and change over time. Because GALVA uses the "LGBTI," this acronym will be used when referencing GALVA material.

the time of writing, this has 3,827 followers (GALVA-108, 2022). Amara das has insisted that Prabhupada did not display discriminatory behavior toward people from the LBGTI community (Wilhelm, 2014). Controversy about same-sex marriage arose when Amara das asked Hridayananda das Goswami about its legitimacy within the Vaishnava tradition. Hridayananda responded that ISKCON should recognize and encourage monogamy among all its members, regardless of orientation, to encourage spiritual sincerity. He added that marriage may not be the best arrangement in all cases, but that "some serious, formal, and public recognition and appreciation of gay monogamy is, in my view, in the best interest of ISKCON and its members" (Hridayananda das Goswami, 2004). This was widely perceived as an endorsement of same-sex marriage and led to heated discussions within the movement. In 2009, Hridayananda das Goswami gave a blessing via email to a same-sex couple's commitment ceremony, which provoked a swift response from the GBC that he must affirm that he upholds "the traditional Krishna conscious view of sex and marriage." Hridayananda did affirm this publicly, but stopped short of stating that his blessing was inappropriate (Venkata Bhatta Dasa, 2009). More recently, a same-sex marriage ceremony was performed in Brazil (Akincana Gocara, 2019), and the issue seems to have died down in online forums in recent years.

In addition to matters of same-sex marriage, dietary practices are currently under consideration. Dairy consumption has been an important part of the Hare Krishna movement, as it is mandated by various scriptural texts that espouse the importance of protecting cows by using their milk, rather than killing them for their meat. In Vaishnava texts, Lord Krishna in Vrindavan is said to be fond of dairy products of all varieties. However, the shift to an increase in plant-based diets and veganism in wider society has also made its way into the Hare Krishna movement. The movement's food distribution project, Food for Life Global, distributes sanctified foods (*prasadam*) to people in impoverished communities and during natural disasters and humanitarian crises. Food for Life only provides grants to affiliate distribution projects that serve vegan foodstuffs, citing the importance of a cruelty-free lifestyle, sustainability, and health and well-being as reasons (Food for Life Global, 2022a). Lestar (2020) studied Hare Krishna communities in Europe and found a significant shift toward veganism prompted by concerns for animal compassion and twenty-first-century factory farming that also negatively impacts dairy animals. This concern is reflected in a catering strategy for outreach activities where several programs and online channels include vegan recipes and cooking presentations. Lestar considers this an unexpected tendency because of the movement's worldview and radical commitment to dairy consumption, arguing that milk and dairy consumption is a nonnegotiable aspect of the movement's theological paradigm. Lestar concludes that compassion for animals and concerns about factory farming override the power of religious orthodoxy and require a reconsideration of the community's norms and values (Lestar, 2020, pp. 817–18).

Online forums including Facebook have been replete with heated debate on the many challenges that the movement has faced in its lifetime. In the last couple of years, new issues have arisen that reflect broader changes in society. Some devotees have expressed their support for Donald Trump and his MAGA ("Make America Great Again") movement which has led to passionate debate with devotees opposed to Donald Trump and his policies. Similarly, the COVID-19 pandemic has given rise to a polarity of views globally regarding the seriousness or even existence of the pandemic and the need for government-mandated lockdowns and vaccination. Those same divisions have been laid bare within the Hare Krishna movement with devotees on different sides of the debate voicing their views, often in rather robust ways. Some devotees have expressed their belief in numerous conspiracy theories and anti-vaccination sentiments, only to have their claims refuted by devotees who deny the credibility of these theories.

Of great concern is the Russo-Ukrainian War, as ISKCON has a significant presence in Ukraine, with fifty-six centers (ISKCON, 2016b) and thousands of devotees. At the time of writing, the Russian invasion of Ukraine is ongoing. At the start of the conflict, devotees in Ukraine were sheltering in place and expressing their intention to carry on with their preaching mission there. Some had left their homes to stay at their local temple and engage in Vaishnava *sanga* (association with devotees), prayer, and *kirtan*. In Hungary, ISKCON centers have received devotees fleeing from Ukraine, and special prayer vigils of *kirtan* for the safety of Ukrainian devotees and people living in Ukraine have taken place in ISKCON communities globally (Anuttama Dasa, 2022). Devotees from Europe, as well as globally, have worked to help devotees from Ukraine with donations (ISKCON News Staff, 2022a) and to find shelter, care, and support through a number of mediums including ISKCON Relief. Temples throughout Europe have offered shelter to devotees fleeing from Ukraine (ISKCON Relief, 2022). The Food for Life food distribution program has been operating in Ukraine to feed victims of the conflict in various parts of the country, including the Donetsk region (Food For Life Global, 2022b). The situation is obviously an evolving one and it remains to be seen what the future holds for the Hare Krishna movement in Ukraine, with large numbers of devotees fleeing to other countries.

It is apparent from social media posts that relations between Russian and Ukrainian Hare Krishna devotees have soured due to the conflict. Ukrainian scholar Michael Sheludko has claimed that the majority of Russian devotees support the government's invasion of Ukraine and have found ways to justify the invasion and encourage Russian soldiers to commit further violence by quoting scriptures. He identifies a narrative among Russian devotees that preventive aggression is justified by the opposition of the spiritless "collective West" to "the spiritual Russian civilization." Ukrainian devotees call for the defense of their country with weapons and criticize those who want to remain neutral, arguing for the need to separate from the Russian control center of the organization.[25] Whether Russian leaders condemn or support Putin's actions determines the attitude of their followers toward them. In short, the pacifist rhetoric that previously characterized the Russian and Ukrainian Vaishnava communities has been replaced with a narrative of violence and division between Russian and Ukrainian devotees (Sheludko, 2022).

Over the years, ISKCON has taken steps to address systemic issues within the institution and, to that end, several agencies have been set up to deal with specific issues, some of which have already been mentioned. The *ISKCON Communications Journal* was established in 1994 to address some of the most challenging issues, including the cult controversy and violations of religious freedom, especially in Eastern Europe. Apart from three sporadic issues, including an attempt to revive it in 2021, it has not been an active publication since 2005 (Smullen, 2021a). As mentioned previously, the Vaishnavi Ministry was established with the aim of increasing equality for women within the movement (Vaishnavi Ministry, 2021) and the Child Protection Office was set up to deal with cases of child abuse (ISKCON Child Protection Office, 2018). In 2002, ISKCON Resolve was established with the assistance of mediation scholar Arnold Zack as a mediation service to help individual members or bodies address and resolve conflict (Zack, 2002). It offers an Ombuds service, mediation services, and self-help tools (ISKCON Resolve, no date) and has helped resolve a number of high-profile conflicts within ISKCON. Vaishnavas CARE is an educational program and support system for patients and loved ones facing acute illness, long-term, chronic illnesses, and end-of-life situations (Vaishnavas CARE, 2020).

Conclusion

Early challenges in the Hare Krishna movement were characterized by disputes with wider society as well as internal disagreements. During the 1970s and 1980s, disputes with wider society were significant due to a lack of cultural

---

[25] Although ISKCON Ukraine is an independent organization, its activities were integrated with those of ISKCON Russia before the Russian invasion of Ukraine. Ukrainian devotees now argue that ISKCON Ukraine needs to be kept separate from ISKCON Russia on an organizational and administrative level.

continuity and frame alignment with host cultures. As tension with wider society reduced, the movement's disputes and controversies became increasingly internal ones. Some issues indicate that the movement has again become more outwardly focused, since they reflect changes in society more broadly. This is apparent in new innovations in proselytization, evolving attitudes toward the LGBTQI+ community, and a shift from the movement's traditional embrace of dairy products toward an increasing embrace of veganism. Attempts to rectify its internal problems indicate ISKCON's willingness to self-reflect as an institution, but these attempts have often been triggered by legal action and negative media coverage. Similarly, fraught relationships with institutions in wider society have prompted an increased desire to align with the norms and expectations of host cultures while working to retain those aspects that are unique to the movement's religious culture, resulting in what Stark would call a medium state of tension with wider society. As ISKCON has increasingly sought to align itself with the expectations and norms of society more broadly, it has become less reactive and more proactive. In the next section I will discuss what this evolving relationship with wider society means for the Hare Krishna movement's future trajectory as a religious movement in the ever-changing world of the twenty-first century.

5 Conclusion: The Hare Krishna Movement in the Twenty-First Century

This section brings together the main themes that have characterized the Hare Krishna movement since its inception. It assesses how the movement is positioned to withstand the current challenges it faces in the context of rapidly changing social, cultural, and political environments and considers its ability to survive and thrive in the twenty-first century. To answer these questions, frame alignment, resource mobilization, and Stark's model are used to assess its current trajectory and whether progressive innovations for remaining relevant in a rapidly changing world are likely to be successful.

Summary of Conclusions

Section 1 introduced the Hare Krishna movement by establishing its theological, cultural, and institutional background. Its formation as a new religious movement in the West, built upon a religious tradition extending back to sixteenth-century West Bengal, defies easy categorization. It is neither a purely ancient religious tradition nor strictly a new religious movement, but, rather, a combination of both. Similarly, the distinction between the Hare Krishna movement and ISKCON as a formal religious institution was made with the caveat that sometimes both conceptions are used interchangeably and sometimes a distinction is made, depending on the context. The movement and the institutional structure of ISKCON were initially one and the same. In the 1970s factions and schisms led to a community of followers beyond the institutional boundaries of ISKCON, and the community has become more diverse due to a complex array of dynamics. Prabhupada understood that his burgeoning movement needed the support of an institutional framework if it was to have any longevity. This is evidenced by the creation of ISKCON in 1966, the year after Prabhupada arrived in the United States to fulfill his mission of spreading Krishna consciousness in the West. Frame alignment was introduced as a way to analyze how the movement evolved with reference to its host cultures. Resource mobilization theory was chosen to interrogate how the movement was able to expand in environments that were not always open to its presence. Stark's model on why new religions succeed and fail served as an analytical lens by which the movement's successes and failures could be understood.

Section 2 examined the beliefs and practices of the Hare Krishna movement, which have their roots in the Gaudiya Vaishnava tradition. Rather than present a textbook account of the daily practices of members of the Hare Krishna movement, the aim was to demonstrate the great variety that exists across the movement, according to followers' levels of commitment and personal identity.

Section 3 discussed the institutional and community dynamics of the Hare Krishna movement. The aim was to provide a way of understanding how Hare Krishna devotees relate to each other in a system of relationships and networks, and how those relational networks provide a context for identity and meaning-making for them. With the caveat that this is not an exhaustive account of the complex set of dynamics that is the Hare Krishna movement, main historical trends in institutional and community dynamics in the movement were identified. Resource mobilization was used to account for the movement's rapid growth in the 1960s and 1970s. It was also used to explain why its proselytization methods and demographic makeup dramatically shifted from a monastic movement, comprised mostly of Western converts in the 1960s, to a congregation-based movement consisting increasingly of followers from Indian-Hindu backgrounds starting in the 1980s. Stark's model helps to explain the movement's changing relationship with and attitude toward wider society. O'Connell's conceptualization of hard, medium, and soft institutions is essential in making the distinction between ISKCON as an institution and the broader Hare Krishna movement. It also allows us to entertain the idea that the movement extends beyond any institutional structure devised to perpetuate the founder's mission. The influence of a changing external environment on the movement's trajectory was also considered. In the twenty-first century, the increasing influence of social media, the reality of climate change, the COVID-19 pandemic, and a rapidly changing geopolitical environment have prompted the movement to adapt its practices and outreach activities.

Section 4 analyzed the most significant challenges and controversies in the movement's history. Disputes with wider society due to a lack of cultural continuity and frame alignment with its host cultures defined the movement's history from the 1960s to the 1980s. As tension with mainstream society relaxed, the movement's disputes increasingly became internal ones. Attempts to rectify internal problems have been significant, but have typically been prompted by legal action and negative media coverage. Adversarial relationships with wider society have gradually led to efforts to align the movement with the expectations of its host cultures, resulting in a medium state of tension with society. This has involved a less reactive and more proactive approach to communication and proselytization. However, it has also required constant adaptation as society changes at an increasing rate. This is evident in new innovations in proselytization, responses to trends in society that include concerns around climate change, and an increased interest in sustainable living, yoga, meditation, and well-being.

Frames and Frame Alignment: A Changing Relationship with Wider Society

Frame alignment and resource mobilization theory provide insight regarding the movement's history until the present. Along with Stark's theoretical framework for why new religions succeed or fail, these frameworks can help project what the movement's future may be. Currently, a complex set of social and geopolitical forces are working to alter the contexts within which the Hare Krishna movement is located, at both local and global levels. While the movement is attempting to respond to these contexts, they are themselves in a rapid state of flux. The Hare Krishna movement started as a drive to change the world by bringing Krishna consciousness to every town and village. Prabhupada claimed on many occasions that this was prophesied by the sixteenth-century saint, Chaitanya, and cited Gaudiya Vaishnava texts to support his claims (Prabhupada, 1971, 2010). Recent attempts to innovate preaching efforts in a rapidly changing world indicate a reactive approach that signifies that the movement is no longer just trying to change the world but is also being changed by it. The question that arises is: to what degree do followers want to change the world, and to what degree do they want to be changed by the world? What balance do they need to strike if the latter is to serve the former?

The Hare Krishna movement's future will depend strongly on what frames it uses. Rochford (2018) points out that, in its infancy, ISKCON aligned with the counterculture and later on with the Indian-Hindu immigrant community. The competing frames of ISKCON as a global preaching organization and as a Hindu movement are at the heart of questions about what path ISKCON should take to be relevant in a rapidly changing world (Rochford, 2018). Some followers and observers of ISKCON see its trajectory as evolving into a Hindu religious organization that has departed from its core mission of preaching to Westerners. However, there is reason to believe this is not the end of the story. Vande Berg and Kniss (2008, p. 80) suggest that Indian immigration has promoted a revival of ISKCON's passion for individual conversion and cultural change. The transition from an unsustainable ashram-based movement to a congregation-based movement got off to a shaky start in the 1980s, as Western converts struggled to make a transition they never expected. However, the entrance of Indian congregation members provided a blueprint for how ISKCON could sustain itself over the long term. Vande Berg and Kniss (2008, p. 91) suggest that Indian involvement in ISKCON has created new opportunities for the reemergence of ISKCON as a religious movement and that Indian devotees are the target and vehicle for that reemergence (Vande Berg and Kniss, 2008, p. 99). Nevertheless, they wonder whether, with increased Indian participation, ISKCON would remain committed to its universalistic movement goals or move toward becoming a more Indian-specific religious and cultural center (Vande Berg and Kniss, 2008, p. 100).

More than a decade after these questions were posed, the emergence of new innovations in preaching gives us reasons to think that this may be a false dichotomy and that the diversity within the movement allows both goals to coexist. The Indian-Hindu community has supported ISKCON through some of its most difficult trials. A joint effort between Westerners and Indian-Hindus would involve a collaborative effort in reenergizing the movement in the twenty-first century. This would require an acknowledgment that both Westerners and Indian-Hindus have a part to play, even if their target audiences and approaches differ.

Many of ISKCON's efforts to continually evolve new frames in its proselytization and recruit new members are a direct reaction to the increased Indianization and Hinduization of ISKCON's temples. The underlying assumption here is that ISKCON is equivalent to its temples. This assumption does not acknowledge the broader Hare Krishna movement, which is comprised of a complex network of relationships among devotees, many of which take place beyond the purview of its temples and official ISKCON events and activities. O'Connell's (2019) conceptualization of the hard, medium, and soft institutions that characterize the Gaudiya Vaishnava tradition is a theoretical foundation for understanding the many levels on which the Hare Krishna movement can be understood. This involves thinking beyond the hard institutional structure of ISKCON to the community of devotees that extends beyond brick-and-mortar temples and official temple programs. The observer may well question the characterization of the Hare Krishna movement as comprising only the hard institutional structure of ISKCON with its management structure, temples, and official ISKCON programs.

Furthermore, a number of new preaching innovations within the movement, most prominently Krishna West, have responded to the perception that the Hare Krishna movement has been completely Indianized and Hinduized and is therefore less likely to attract Westerners – a cornerstone of Prabhupada's mission. For this reason, presenting Krishna consciousness in line with Western cultural tastes is foundational to this preaching initiative. This approach echoes Stark's proposition that religious movements will succeed to the extent that they retain cultural continuity with the conventional faiths of the societies in which they operate (Stark, 1996, p. 136). While associating only with other devotees was emphasized in the early days of the movement, interaction with outsiders for the purposes of recruiting them into the mission was necessary for the movement to grow. Stark has argued that religious movements will be successful if they sustain strong internal attachments, but also remain an open social network that can establish and maintain ties to outsiders (Stark, 1996, pp. 142–3). As the movement has transitioned from a monastic ashram-based religion to a diverse network of followers who work and study outside the movement, the challenge has been to maintain strong internal attachments. As relationships with nondevotees become more important, and the distinction between insiders and outsiders starts to break down for some followers, their commitment to the mission may start to wane. It is here that festivals and online forums where devotees can associate with each other become important. New and innovative preaching initiatives can reenergize followers to engage in the preaching mission set by Prabhupada. For this reason, these new initiatives are important not only for bringing in newcomers. They may also help in maintaining relationships with followers whose links to the movement are compromised by a lack of enthusiasm or resentment over disputes, as well as those who do not have family members and children who are devotees, and who can keep them tied to the movement.

As the movement's new preaching initiatives seek to attract new members, the question arises as to whether this is feasible in an age of religious seeking where younger seekers want to have an experience of spirituality but without high levels of commitment to a religion. Some sociologists have characterized the contemporary context where there is a variety of choice as a "spiritual supermarket" (Roof, 2001). As Mason, Singleton, and Webber (2007, p. 156) point out, the spiritual marketplace accommodates eclecticism, where consumers can select "unbundled" components of spirituality rather than having to buy a complete package. Heelas and Woodhead (2005) argue that the "spiritual revolution" indicates an increasing reluctance among Western populations to live life according to religious authority, and the desire instead to embark on a personal journey of discovering the sacred. In this way, they suggest that new forms of spirituality are overtaking traditional forms of participating in organized religion. Partridge (2005) argues that contemporary Western spiritualities are emerging that are different from declining traditional religions and are fed by popular culture. Carrette (2013) maintains that spirituality has become a commodity in the global marketplace and embodies the privatization of religion in the modern West. It is conceivable that innovators of new preaching initiatives in the Hare Krishna movement become so adept at competing in the spiritual marketplace that they lose sight of the core messages that sustain the religious mission established by its founder.

Karapanagiotis (2021) has identified the different assumptions underlying the various approaches taken in trying to rebrand the Hare Krishna movement for a Western audience. The loft preaching program initiated by Devamrita Swami sees lofts as an entry point for newcomers that directs them to ISKCON temples as the ultimate destination. Hridayananda das Goswami's Krishna West program, by contrast, does not see temples as the final destination. If Krishna consciousness is the ultimate goal for followers, rather than engaging in a particular physical space, it may not really matter whether people attend a temple or not. Attendance at the temple is, however, assumed by some devotees to be an important way of associating with other devotees. Part of the reason is because attendance at temple services and worshipping the deity in the temple are primary ways of practicing Krishna consciousness according to *Bhakti-rasamrta-sindhu*. However, attention to the ways of practicing Krishna consciousness in their totality, as outlined in *Bhakti-rasamrta-sindhu*, may lead to an understanding that different modes of participation within the Hare Krishna movement can coexist, rather than competing with each other or negating each other.

The challenge for the Hare Krishna movement is to adapt to a rapidly changing world while remaining true to the core values unique to its religious tradition: in Stark's words, to offer a religious culture that sets it apart from the general, secular culture, to be distinctive, and impose relatively strict moral standards while maintaining a medium level of tension with its surrounding environment – to be strict, but not too strict (Stark, 1996, p. 137). The move-ment's willingness to adapt to the changing values and trends in mainstream society is indicated by such shifts as branding several ISKCON farm commu-nities as ecovillages, increasingly moving from dairy consumption toward veganism, and ISKCON centers that proactively complied with public health orders during the COVID-19 pandemic. These are shifts that indicate an increasing alignment with mainstream society.

Dealing with Internal Issues

Internal issues will continue to need attention. Although ISKCON as an institu-tion is focused on the ways in which it can adapt its proselytization efforts to a changing world, it continues to be internally focused on disputes including leadership and authority, the position and role of women, and female gurus. This inward focus impacts its ability to be externally directed and reach new audi-ences – and thus engage in its original missionizing objectives set by Prabhupada. Stark proposes that religious movements will be successful to the degree that they have legitimate leaders with enough authority to be effect-ive, and this in turn depends upon clear doctrinal justifications for an effective and legitimate leadership (Stark, 1996, p. 139). Spiritual leadership of ISKCON has been plagued by concerns about its legitimacy, based on questions about whether it is in line with Prabhupada's wishes, and this has been exposed in debates around the issue of succession. The lack of trust in leadership has been exacerbated by allegations of leader malfeasance, including child abuse and sexual misconduct among some of ISKCON's gurus. The longevity of the movement in the twenty-first century relies to some degree upon the leadership transparently addressing issues of misconduct in their ranks and consulting with stakeholders, including victims of abuse and ISKCON's membership, in this process.

The Future of the Hare Krishna Movement
in the Twenty-First Century

A key challenge for the Hare Krishna movement in the twenty-first century will be how to mobilize resources and adapt to changing circumstances as it has done in the past. Stark argues that if religious movements are to grow, they need a highly motivated, volunteer labor force, including many willing to proselytize (Stark, 1996, p. 140). Maintaining the ISKCON temples that were acquired when book distribution by a large full-time volunteer labor force was the key form of resource mobilization is a significant challenge. Addressing this chal-lenge involves thinking about the use of such centers and considering whether devotees should live there, what events should be held, and whether centers should continue to be largely maintained by an Indian and Hindu congregation. If current ISKCON temples are not to be the main venue for outreach to Westerners, what spaces will be used for outreach and who will fund such spaces? Should outreach take place in the residences of followers, instead, to minimize costs? These are central questions around how resource mobilization is to be achieved in a dramatically altered internal and external environment.

The Hare Krishna movement's future trajectory as a religious movement in the twenty-first century is largely dependent on decisions about what frames its members want to align it with. The perception that the movement is evolving from its original mission of being a global preaching organization to a Hindu movement will need to be resolved, along with addressing whether both aspects can be maintained within the same movement. If they can, what spaces will they occupy within ISKCON's infrastructure of temple communities? New preaching innovations are a sign that the movement is attempting to adapt to the dynamic social and cultural environments of the twenty-first century. The reality that relationship networks of followers have found a new space in the online environment is a sign that the dispersion of once close geographically bound relationships can benefit from an increasingly virtual world. The movement's response to concerns around climate change in the form of ecovillages and veganism, and the growing interest in yoga, meditation, and well-being in the wider society indicates that the movement can adapt to a dramatically changing external environment. The challenge will be to adapt to these changes while remaining faithful to the core beliefs and practices of Krishna consciousness and maintaining meaningful relationships among devotees and, at the same time, forging new relationships in wider society. If this balance can be struck, the movement has a good chance of surviving throughout and beyond the twenty-first century.

References

Akincana Gocara. (2019). "ISKCON Performs the First Hare Krishna Gay Marriage Ceremony in Brazil." *AS IT IS*, October 24. https://rfranco1008 .blogspot.com/2019/10/iskcon-performs-first-hare-krishna-gay.html.

Anderson, J. (1986). "The Hare Krishna Movement in the USSR." *Religion in Communist Lands* 14(3), 316–17.

Associated Press. (1996). "Ex-Hare Krishna Leader Gets 20-Year Sentence." *New York Times*, August 29. www.nytimes.com/1996/08/29/us/ex-hare-krishna-leader-gets-20-year-sentence.html.

Back To Godhead. (1995). "Persecution in Armenia!" *Back To Godhead*, July 1. www.backtogodhead.in/persecution-in-armenia/.

BBC News. (2011). "Russia Court Declares Hindu Book Bhagvad Gita Legal." *BBC News*, December 28. www.bbc.com/news/world-asia-india-16344615.

BBT Trustees. (2008). "BBT Statement on Annotating Srila Prabhupada's Books." *ISKCON News*, July 2. https://iskconnews.org/bbt-statement-on-annotating-srila-prabhupadas-books/.

Bhaktivedanta Book Trust. (2012). "Controversies." http://bbtedit.com/controversies.

Bhaktivedanta Book Trust International, Inc. (no date). "Bhaktivedanta Vedabase." https://vedabase.io/en/.

Bhaktivedanta Institute. (2021). "About Us." http://binstitute.org/bhaktivedanta-institute/.

Blumetti, J. (2019). "'It's Latent Misogyny': Hare Krishnas Divided over Whether to Allow Female Gurus." *Guardian*, June 4. www.theguardian .com/world/2019/jun/04/hare-krishna-india-hinduism-florida-women.

Bromley, D. G. and Melton, J. G. (2012). "Reconceptualizing Types of Religious Organization: Dominant, Sectarian, Alternative, and Emergent Tradition Groups." *Nova Religio* 15(3), 4–28. https://doi.org/10.1525/nr.2012.15.3.4.

Broo, M. (2003). *As Good as God: The Guru in Gaudiya Vaisnavism*. Åbo, Finland: Åbo Akademi University Press.

Bryant, E. F. and Ekstrand, M. L. (2004). *The Hare Krishna Movement: The Postcharismatic Fate of a Religious Transplant*. New York, NY: Columbia University Press.

Buniatyan, G. and Buniatyan, S. (2007). *Salted Bread: A True Story*. Badger, CO: Torchlight Publishing.

Burt, A. R. (2013). "Leading the Hare Krishna Movement: The Crisis of Succession in the International Society for Krishna Consciousness, 1977–1987." Ph.D. thesis. University of Leeds.

Burt, A. R. (2019). "An Uncertain Future: The Issue of Succession in the International Society for Krishna Consciousness." In K. Knott and M. Francis, eds., *Minority Religions and Uncertainty*. Abingdon, UK: Routledge, pp. 86–99.

Čargonja, H. (2022). "Realisations, Arrangements, and Ecstasies: Narratives of Religious Experience in the Hare Kṛṣṇa Movement." *Journal of Hindu Studies* 15(2), 121–47. https://doi.org/10.1093/jhs/hiac005.

Carrette, J. (2013). *Selling Spirituality: The Silent Takeover of Religion*. Hoboken, NJ: Taylor & Francis.

Chatterji, A. P., Hansen, T. B., and Jaffrelot, C. (2019). *Majoritarian State: How Hindu Nationalism Is Changing India*. Oxford: Oxford University Press. https://doi.org/10.1093/oso/9780190078171.001.0001.

Court of Appeal, Fourth District, Division 1, California. (1992). *George v. International Society for Krishna Consciousness of California*. https://caselaw.findlaw.com/ca-court-of-appeal/1775782.html.

Crnic, A. (2009). "Cult versus Church Religiosity: Comparative Study of Hare Krishna Devotees and Catholics in Slovenia." *Social Compass* 56(1), 117–35. https://doi.org/10.1177/0037768608100346.

Daner, F. J. (1976). *The American Children of Krishna: A Study of the Hare Krishna Movement*. New York, NY: Holt, Rinehart & Winston.

Das, Achyutananda. (2012). *Blazing Sadhus*. CMB Books.

Das, Kalyana Giriraj. (2022). "Omicron Variant of Corona Virus Hits ISKCON Temples." *ISKCON News*, January 8. https://iskconnews.org/omicron-variant-of-corona-virus-hits-iskcon-temples/.

Das, R. P. (1996). "'Vedic' in the Terminology of Prabhupada and His Followers." *ISKCON Communications Journal* 4(2). http://content.iskcon.org/icj/4_2/4_2vedic.html.

Dasa, Ajit Krishna. (no date). "About." Arsa-Prayoga: Can We Change Srila Prabhupada's Books? https://arsaprayoga.com/about/.

Dasa, Anuttama. (2022). "Devotees in Ukraine Continue on Despite Fears, Instability." *ISKCON News*, February 25. https://iskconnews.org/devotees-in-ukraine-continue-on-despite-fears-instability/.

Dasa, Madhudvisa. (1998). "Is ISKCON Editing or Changing Prabhupada's Books?" *BookChanges*.com. https://bookchanges.com/is-iskcon-editing-or-changing-prabhupada%e2%80%99s-books/.

Dasa, Ravindra Svarupa. (2014). *Srila Prabhupada: The Founder-Acarya of ISKCON*. ISKCON GBC Press. www.founderacharya.com/book/.

Dasa, Satyanarayana and Dasa, Kundali. (2019). *In Vaikuntha Not Even the Leaves Fall: A Treatise on the Bondage of the Jiva*. Vrindavan, India: Jiva Institute of Vaishnava Studies.

Dasa, Shukavak. (1986). "The Problem of Apostasy in Krishna Consciousness." *Vaishnava Journal* 1(3–4), 39–42. http://www.prabhupada-connect.com/VJ-3.pdf.

Dasa, Venkata Bhatta. (2009). "Hridayananda Goswami Clarifies Position on Sex and Marriage." *ISKCON News*, April 18. https://iskconnews.org/hridaya nanda-goswami-clarifies-position-on-sex-and-marriage/.

Dasi, Kumari Kunti and Das, Madan Gopal. (2022). "Narayani Devi Dasi Initiates Her First Diksa Disciple." *ISKCON News*, August 23. https://iskcon news.org/narayani-devi-dasi-initiates-her-first-diksa-disciple/.

Dasi, Visakha. (2000). "Women in ISKCON." *ISKCON Communications Journal* 8(1). https://content.iskcon.org/icj/8_1/visakha.html.

Davie, G. (1990). "Believing without Belonging: Is This the Future of Religion in Britain?" *Social Compass* 37(4), 455–69. https://doi.org/10.1177/003776890037004004.

Desai, K. (1996). *The Final Order.* www.iskconirm.com/docs/pdf/tfo.pdf.

Devi Dasi, Radha. (1998). "Participation, Protection and Patriarchy: An International Model for the Role of Women in ISKCON." *ISKCON Communications Journal* 6(1). https://content.iskcon.org/icj/6_1/6_1radha .html.

Dines, M. (2015). "The Sacralization of Straightedge Punk: Bhakti-yoga, Nada Brahma and the Divine Received Embodiment of Krishnacore." *Muzikološki Zbornik* 50(2), 147–56. https://doi.org/10.4312/mz.50.2.147-156.

Dwyer, G. and Cole, R. J., eds. (2007). *The Hare Krishna Movement: Forty Years of Chant and Change.* London: I. B. Tauris.

Dwyer, G. and Cole, R. J., eds. (2013). *Hare Krishna in the Modern World.* London: Arktos.

Ebaugh, H. R. (2004). "Religion across Borders: Transnational Religious Ties." *Asian Journal of Social Science* 32(2), 216–31. https://doi.org/10.1163/1568531041705086.

Eidson, J. R., Feyissa, D., Fuest, V. et al. (2017). "From Identification to Framing and Alignment: A New Approach to the Comparative Analysis of Collective Identities." *Current Anthropology* 58(3), 340–59. https://doi.org/10.1086/691970.

Eremenko, A. (2014). "Persecuted by Soviets, Russia's Hare Krishnas Still Fight for Acceptance (Video)." *Moscow Times*, July 11. www.themoscow times.com/2014/07/11/persecuted-by-soviets-russias-hare-krishnas-still-fight-for-acceptance-video-a37234.

Fahy, J. (2017). "Failing Well: Accommodating Vices in an Ideal Vedic City." *HAU Journal of Ethnographic Theory* 7(2), 331–50. https://doi.org/10.14318/hau7.2.030.

Fahy, J. (2018). "The Constructive Ambiguity of Vedic Culture in ISKCON Mayapur." *Journal of Hindu Studies* 11(3), 234–59. https://doi.org/10.1093/jhs/hiy008.

Fahy, J. (2019a). *Becoming Vaishnava in an Ideal Vedic City.* New York, NJ: Berghahn Books.

Fahy, J. (2019b). "Learning to Love Krishna: A Living Theology of Moral Emotions." *Ethnos* 84(1), 142–59. https://doi.org/10.1080/00141844.2017.1383500.

Farkas, J. (2021). "Eco Valley or New Vraja Dham? Competing Emic Interpretations of the Hungarian Krishna Valley." *Religions* 12(8), 1–19. https://doi.org/10.3390/rel12080622.

Food for Life Global. (2022a). "About Food for Life Global." Website. https://ffl.org/.

Food for Life Global. (2022b). "Response to Crisis in Ukraine," March 1. https://ffl.org/projects/response-to-crisis-in-ukraine/.

Fox, M. (2011). "Swami Bhaktipada, Ex-Hare Krishna Leader, Dies at 74." *New York Times*, October 24. www.nytimes.com/2011/10/25/us/swami-bhaktipada-ex-hare-krishna-leader-dies-at-74.html.

Freeman, J. (1979). "Resource Mobilization and Strategy." In M. N. Zald and J. D. McCarthy, eds., *The Dynamics of Social Movements: Resource Mobilization, Social Control and Tactics.* Cambridge, MA: Winthrop Publishers, pp. 167–89.

Fuller, J. D. (2005). "Reading, Writing, and Reclaiming: Bhaktivinoda Thakura and the Modernization of Gaudiya Vaishnavism." *Journal of Vaishnava Studies* 13, 75–94.

GALVA-108. (2022). Gay and Lesbian Vaishnava Association (GALVA-108). Facebook page. www.facebook.com/galva108/.

GALVA-108. (no date). "About GALVA-108." www.galva108.org/about-galva-108.

Goffman, E. (1974). *Frame Analysis: An Essay on the Organization of Experience.* 1st ed. Cambridge, MA: Harvard University Press.

Goswami, Satsvarupa das. (1980a). *Srila Prabhupada-lilamrta, Volume 1.* Bhaktivedanta Vedabase. https://vedabase.io/en/library/spl/1/.

Goswami, Satsvarupa das. (1980b). *Srila Prabhupada-lilamrta, Volume 2.* Bhaktivedanta Vedabase. https://vedabase.io/en/library/spl/2/.

Goswami, Satsvarupa das. (1993a). *Srila Prabhupada-Lilamrta: A Biography of His Divine Grace A. C. Bhaktivedanta Swami Prabhupada. A Lifetime in Preparation, India 1896–1965.* Mumbai: Bhaktivedanta Book Trust.

Goswami, Satsvarupa das. (1993b). *Srila Prabhupada-Lilamrta: A Biography of His Divine Grace A. C. Bhaktivedanta Swami Prabhupada. Only He Could Lead Them, San Francisco/India 1967*. Mumbai: Bhaktivedanta Book Trust.

Goswami, Satsvarupa das. (1993c). *Srila Prabhupada-Lilamrta: A Biography of His Divine Grace A. C. Bhaktivedanta Swami Prabhupada. Planting the Seed, New York City 1965–66*. Mumbai: Bhaktivedanta Book Trust.

Goswami, Satsvarupa das. (1993d). *Srila Prabhupada-Lilamrta: A Biography of His Divine Grace A. C. Bhaktivedanta Swami Prabhupada, Uniting Two Worlds 1975–77*. Mumbai: Bhaktivedanta Book Trust.

Goswami, Tamal Krishna. (1997). "The Perils of Succession: Heresies of Authority and Continuity in the Hare Krishna Movement." *ISKCON Communications Journal* 5(1). https://content.iskcon.org/icj/5_1/5_1perils.html.

Goswami, Tamal Krishna. (1999). *TKG's Diary: Prabhupada's Final Days*. 2nd ed. Dallas, TX: Pundits Press.

Goswami, Tamal Krishna. (2012). *A Living Theology of Krishna Bhakti: Essential Teachings of A. C. Bhaktivedanta Swami Prabhupada*. Edited by G. M. Schweig. New York: Oxford University Press.

Govinda Valley. (no date). "Who We Are." Website. www.govindavalley.com .au/who-we-are.

Greene, J. M. (2016). *Swami in a Strange Land: How Krishna Came to the West*. San Rafael, CA: Mandala Publishing.

Gusfield, J. (1981). "Social Movements and Social Change: Perspectives of Linearity and Fluidity." In L. Kriesberg, ed., *Research in Social Movements, Conflict and Change*. Greenwich, CT: JAI Press, pp. 317–39.

Haddon, M. (2013a). "Anthropological Proselytism: Reflexive Questions for a Hare Krishna Ethnography." *Australian Journal of Anthropology* 24(3), 250–69. https://doi.org/10.1111/taja.12050.

Haddon, M. (2013b). "Old, New, Borrowed, Blue: ISKCON's Troubled History with Gaudiya Vaisnavism." *Alternative Spirituality and Religion Review* 4(2), 218–32.

Haddon, M. (2013c). "Speaking of Krishna: Rhetoric and Revelation in the International Society for Krishna Consciousness (ISKCON)." *Alternative Spirituality and Religion Review* 4(1), 49–69. https://doi.org/10.5840/ asrr20134118.

Hall, D. D. (1997). "Introduction." In D. D. Hall, ed., *Lived Religion in America: Toward a History of Practice*. Princeton, NJ: Princeton University Press, pp. vii–xiv.

Hatton, T. J. (2015). "United States Immigration Policy: The 1965 Act and its Consequences." *Scandinavian Journal of Economics* 117(2), 347–68. https:// doi.org/10.1111/sjoe.12094.

Heelas, P. and Woodhead, L., eds. (2005). *The Spiritual Revolution: Why Religion Is Giving Way to Spirituality*. Oxford: Blackwell.

Hopkins, T. J. (1989). "The Social and Religious Background for Transmission of Gaudiya Vaishnavism to the West." In D. G. Bromley and L. D. Shinn, eds., *Krishna Consciousness in the West*. Lewisburg, PA: Bucknell University Press, pp. 35–54.

Hopkins, T. J. (1998). "Why Should ISKCON Study Its own History?" *ISKCON Communications Journal* 6(2). https://content.iskcon.org/icj/6_2/62hopkins .html.

Hopkins, T. J. (1999). "Why Should ISKCON Study its own History? (Addendum)." *ISKCON Communications Journal* 7(1). https://content.isk con.org/icj/7_1/71hopkins.html.

Hridayananda das Goswami. (2004). "Gay Monogamy by Hridayananda dasa Goswami." ISKCON Media Vedic Library. https://sites.google.com/a/iskconme dia.com/docs/controversial/gay-monogamy-by-hridayananda-dasa-goswami.

Introvigne, M. (1997). "Religious Liberty in Western Europe." *ISKCON Communications Journal* 5(2). https://content.iskcon.org/icj/5_2/5_2liberty .html.

Introvigne, M. (2021). "Russia Hit by European Court for Discriminating Krishnas, Unification Church," November 29. https://bitterwinter.org/rus sia-hit-by-european-court/.

ISKCON. (2016a). "Govardhan Eco Village Maharashtra, ISKCON Centres." Website. https://centres.iskcon.org/centre/govardhan-eco-village-maharashtra/.

ISKCON. (2016b). "ISKCON Centres: The Official Global Directory of Temples and Other Centres in the International Society for Krishna Consciousness." https://centres.iskcon.org/.

ISKCON Child Protection Office. (2018). "ISKCON Child Protection Office, History." Website www.iskconchildprotection.org/-about.

ISKCON Communications Europe. (1994). "Persecution of Hare Krishna Members in Armenia." *ISKCON Communications Journal* 2(2). https://con tent.iskcon.org/icj/2_2/armenia.html.

ISKCON Communications Journal. (1995). "Update on the Repression of Religious Freedom in Armenia." *ISKCON Communications Journal* 3(1). https://content.iskcon.org/icj/3_1/ice.html.

ISKCON GBC. (2019). "GBC Approves Vaishnavi Diksa Gurus in ISKCON." *ISKCON News*, October 18. https://iskconnews.org/gbc-approves-vaishnavi-diksa-gurus-in-iskcon/.

ISKCON GBC. (2022a). "Female Diksa Guru." https://gbc.iskcon.org/female-diksa-guru/.

ISKCON GBC. (2022b). "List of Initiating Gurus in ISKCON." https://gbc .iskcon.org/list-of-initiating-gurus-in-iskcon/.

ISKCON GBC. (2022c). "Members' Profiles." https://gbc.iskcon.org/mem bers-profile/.

ISKCON GBC Executive Committee. (2008). "GBC Statement Reaffirms Vaishnava Respect for Women." *ISKCON News*, May 29. https://iskcon news.org/gbc-statement-reaffirms-vaishnava-respect-for-women/.

ISKCON GBC Press. (1996). *Our Original Position*. Bhaktivedanta Book Trust.

ISKCON Governing Body Commission. (1977). "GBC Meets with Srila Prabhupada." Bhaktivedanta Archives, Sandy Ridge, NC.

ISKCON Governing Body Commission. (1978). "GBC Resolutions."

ISKCON Governing Body Commission. (1987). "GBC Resolutions."

ISKCON Governing Body Commission. (1988). "GBC Resolutions."

ISKCON Governing Body Commission. (2015). "Joint Statement from the GBC and Hridayananda Das Goswami," March 17. https://gbc.iskcon.org/ statement-regarding-krishna-west/.

ISKCON News. (2013). "Moscow May Lose Its Sole Hare Krishna Temple." *ISKCON News*, August 2. https://iskconnews.org/moscow-may-lose-its-sole-hare-krishna-temple/.

ISKCON News. (2021). "GBC Amends and Affirms Law Allowing Vaisnavis to Initiate." *ISKCON News*, December 22. https://iskconnews.org/gbc-amends-and-affirms-law-allowing-vaisnavis-to-initiate/.

ISKCON News Staff. (2022a). "UPDATED: Verified Donations for Ukraine." *ISKCON News*, April 28. https://iskconnews.org/verified-donations-for-ukraine/.

ISKCON News Staff. (2022b). "GBC Pauses Vaishnavi Diksa Gurus, Again." *ISKCON News*, December 23. https://iskconnews.org/gbc-pauses-vaishnavi-diksa-gurus-again/.

ISKCON Relief. (2022). "ISKCON Relief Ukraine Report Week 16," June 22. http://iskconrelief.org/iskcon-relief-ukraine-report-week-16/.

ISKCON Resolve. (no date). "Our Services." Website. www.iskconresolve.org/ services.

ISKCON Revival Movement. (2022a). Website. www.iskconirm.com.

ISKCON Revival Movement. (2022b). Facebook page. www.facebook.com/ iskconirm/.

ISKCON Revival Movement. (2022c). "Back to Prabhupada." Twitter. https:// twitter.com/iskconIRM

ISKCON Revival Movement. (2022d). "FAQ." Website. www.iskconirm.com/ faq1/.

Jakupko, D. V. (1986). "The Persecution of the Hare Krishna Movement in the U. S. S. R." www.hkussr.com/hkdoc01sec1p1.htm.

Jenkins, J. C. (1983). "Resource Mobilization Theory and the Study of Social Movements." *Annual Review of Sociology* 9, 527–53.

Jones, C. and Ryan, J. D. (2006). *Encyclopedia of Hinduism*. New York, NY: Facts On File.

Judah, S. (1974). *Hare Krishna and the Counterculture*. New York, NY: John Wiley & Sons.

Kamarás, I. (1999). "Devotees of Krishna in Hungary." *ISKCON Communications Journal* 7(2). https://content.iskcon.org/icj/7_2/72kamaras.html.

Karapanagiotis, N. (2021). *Branding Bhakti: Krishna Consciousness and the Makeover of a Movement*. Bloomington: Indiana University Press.

Ketola, K. (2008). *The Founder of the Hare Krishnas as Seen by Devotees: A Cognitive Study of Religious Charisma*. Leiden: Brill.

Knott, K. (1986). *My Sweet Lord: The Hare Krishna Movement*. Wellingborough, UK: The Aquarian Press.

Knott, K. (1993). "Contemporary Theological Trends in the Hare Krsna Movement: A Theology of Religions." *ISKCON Communications Journal* 1(1). https://content.iskcon.org/icj/1_1/knott.html.

Knott, K. (1994). "Problems in the Interpretation of Vedic Literature: The Perennial Battle between the Scholar and the Devotee." *ISKCON Communications Journal* 1(2). https://content.iskcon.org/icj/1_2/12knott.html.

Knott, K. (1995a). "Insider and Outsider Perceptions of Prabhupada." *ISKCON Communications Journal* 5(1). https://content.iskcon.org/icj/5_1/5_1knott.html.

Knott, K. (1995b). "Recent Statements about ISKCON." *ISKCON Communications Journal* 3(1). https://content.iskcon.org/icj/3_1/knott.html.

Knott, K. (1995c). "The Debate about Women in the Hare Krishna Movement." *ISKCON Communications Journal* 3(2). https://content.iskcon.org/icj/3_2/3_2knott.html.

Knott, K. (2004). "Healing the Heart of ISKCON: The Place of Women." In E. F. Bryant and M. L. Ekstrand, eds., *The Hare Krishna Movement: The Postcharismatic Fate of a Religious Transplant*. New York, NY: Columbia University Press, pp. 291–311.

Kramer, S. (2021). "Key Findings about the Religious Composition of India." *Pew Research Center*, September 21. www.pewresearch.org/fact-tank/2021/09/21/key-findings-about-the-religious-composition-of-india/.

Lawrence, B. B. (2002). *New Faiths, Old Fears: Muslims and Other Asian Immigrants in American Religious Life*. New York, NY: Columbia University Press. https://doi.org/10.7312/lawr11520.

Leman, J. and Roos, H. (2007). "The Process of Growth in Krishna Consciousness and Sacredness in Belgium." *Journal of Contemporary Religion* 22(3), 327–40. https://doi.org/10.1080/13537900701637486.

Lestar, T. (2018). "Disconnecting from Technology on Hare Krishna Farms." *Human Geography* 11(3), 43–56. https://doi.org/10.1177/1942778618011 00304.

Lestar, T. (2020). "Religions Going Nuts? Faith-Based Veganism and Transformative Learning in the Context of Sustainability Transitions (Case 1: The Hare Krishna Movement)." *Journal of Organizational Change Management* 33(5), 805–19. https://doi.org/10.1108/JOCM-09-2019-0274.

Lewis, J. R. and Lewis, S. M., eds. (2009). *Sacred Schisms: How Religions Divide*. New York, NY: Cambridge University Press.

Lilamayi Gaurangi. (2015). "The Reassertion of Women Within ISKCON: Vaishnavis and Their Critics." *ISKCON Vaishnavi Ministry*, May 8. https://vaishnaviministry.org/the-reassertion-of-women-within-iskcon-vaishnavis-and-their-critics/.

Loiwal, M. (2020). "Bengal: Iskcon Rath Yatra Goes digital, Will Cover 6 Continents in 24 Hours Tomorrow." *India Today*, June 22. www.indiatoday .in/india/story/bengal-mayapur-iskcon-rath-yatra-digital-continents-1691525-2020-06-22.

Lucia, A. (2015). "How ISKCON Took Hinduism to the US Heartland." *Scroll. in*, January 17. https://scroll.in. http://scroll.in/article/700557/how-iskcon-took-hinduism-to-the-us-heartland.

Madsen, F. (2000). "Asrama, Yukta-vairagya et Structure d'organisation de l'ISKCON." *Social Compass* 47(2), 187–204. https://doi.org/10.1177/ 003776800047002004.

Mason, M., Singleton, A., and Webber, R. (2007). "The Spirituality of Young Australians." *International Journal of Children's Spirituality* 12(2), 149–63. https://doi.org/10.1080/13644360701467451.

McCarthy, J. D. and Zald, M. N. (1977). "Resource Mobilization and Social Movements: A Partial Theory." *American Journal of Sociology* 82(6), 1212–41. https://doi.org/10.1086/226464.

McCutcheon, R. T., ed. (1999). *The Insider/Outsider Problem in the Study of Religion: A Reader*. London: Cassell.

McGuire, M. B. (2008). *Lived Religion: Faith and Practice in Everyday Life*. New York, NY: Oxford University Press. https://academic.oup.com/book/3374.

Melton, J. G. (1987). "How New Is New? The Flowering of the 'New' Religious Consciousness since 1965." In D. G. Bromley and P. E. Hammond, eds., *The Future of New Religious Movements*. Macon, GA: Mercer University Press, pp. 46–56.

Melton, J. G. (2004). "Perspective: Toward a Definition of 'New Religion'." *Nova Religio* 8(1), 73–87. https://doi.org/10.1525/nr.2004.8.1.73.

Melton, J. G. (2007a). "Introducing and Defining the Concept of a New Religion." In D. G. Bromley, ed., *Teaching New Religious Movements*. New York, NY: Oxford University Press, pp. 29–40.

Melton, J. G. (2007b). "Perspective: New New Religions: Revisiting a Concept." *Nova Religio* 10(4), 103–12. https://doi.org/10.1525/nr.2007.10.4.103.

Mitsuhara, T. V. (2019). "Moving Toward Utopia: Language, Empathy, and Chastity among Mobile Mothers and Children in Mayapur, West Bengal." Ph.D. thesis. University of California–Los Angeles.

Mukunda Goswami. (1995). "NRM Is a Four-Letter Word: The Language of Oppression." *ISKCON Communications Journal* 3(2), 73–5. https://content.iskcon.org/icj/3_2/3_2 mg.html.

Muster, N. J. (2004). "Life as a Woman on Watseka Avenue: Personal Story I." In E. F. Bryant and M. L. Ekstrand, eds., *The Hare Krishna Movement: The Postcharismatic Fate of a Religious Transplant*. New York, NY: Columbia University Press, pp. 312–20.

New Vrindaban. (2021a). "History." Website. www.newvrindaban.com/history.

New Vrindaban. (2021b). "Your Visit." Website.www.newvrindaban.com/your-visit.

Nye, M. (1996). "Hare Krishna and Sanatan Dharm in Britain: The Campaign for Bhaktivedanta Manor." *Journal of Contemporary Religion* 11(1), 37–56. https://doi.org/10.1080/13537909608580754.

Nye, M. (1998). "Minority Religious Groups and Religious Freedom in England: The ISKCON Temple at Bhaktivedanta Manor." *Journal of Church and State* 40(2), 411–36. https://doi.org/10.1093/jcs/40.2.411.

Nye, M. (2001). *Multiculturalism and Minority Religions in Britain: Krishna Consciousness, Religious Freedom and the Politics of Location*. London: Routledge.

O'Connell, J. T. (2019). "Institutionalizing Prema-Bhakti." In J. T. O'Connell and R. Lutjeharms, eds., *Caitanya Vaiṣṇavism in Bengal: Social Impact and Historical Implications*. Abingdon, UK: Routledge, pp. 27–49.

Orchowski, M. S. (2015). *The Law That Changed the Face of America: The Immigration and Nationality Act of 1965*. Lanham, MD: Rowman & Littlefield.

Orsi, R. A. (2002). *The Madonna of 115th Street: Faith and Community in Italian Harlem, 1880–1950*. New Haven, CT: Yale University Press.

Partridge, C. H. (2005). *The Re-Enchantment of the West: Alternative Spiritualities, Sacralization, Popular Culture, and Occulture*. London: T & T Clark.

84   *References*

Persson, A. (2019). *Framing Social Interaction: Continuities and Cracks in Goffman's Frame Analysis.* London: Routledge. https://doi.org/10.4324/9781315582931.

Petrova, M. (2013). "Underground Hindu and Buddhist-Inspired Religious Movements in Soviet Russia." *Usuteaduslik Ajakiri* 1(63), 99–115.

Prabhupada, A. C. B. S. (1971). *Caitanya-bhāgavata, Antya-khaṇḍa 4.126.* Los Angeles. https://vedabase.io/en/library/transcripts/710702cb-los-angeles/.

Prabhupada, A. C. B. S. (1976). "Letter to: All Governing Board Commissioners." Bhaktivedanta Vedabase, May 19. https://vedabase.io/en/library/letters/letter-to-all-governing-board-commissioners/.

Prabhupada, A. C. B. S. (1977). *Srimad-Bhagavatam.* Bhaktivedanta Book Trust International, Inc. https://vedabase.io/en/library/sb/3/20/26/?query=homosexual#bb24381.

Prabhupada, A. C. B. S. (1992). *Srila Prabhupada Siksamrta: Nectarian Instructions from the Letters of His Divine Grace A. C. Bhaktivedanta Swami Prabhupada.* Los Angeles: Bhaktivedanta Book Trust.

Prabhupada, A. C. B. S. (2010). *Bhagavad-gita As It Is.* E-book. Bhaktivedanta Book Trust.

Prabhupada, A. C. B. S. (2011). *The Nectar of Instruction.* E-book. Bhaktivedanta Book Trust.

Prabhupada, A. C. B. S. (2012). *The Nectar of Devotion: The Complete Science of Bhakti-Yoga.* E-book. Bhaktivedanta Book Trust.

Prabhupada, A. C. B. S. and Goswami, Tamal Krishna. (1977). "Room Conversation." Bhaktivedanta Vedabase, July 7. https://vedabase.io/en/library/transcripts/770707r1vrn/.

Pranskevičiūtė, R. and Juras, T. (2014). "Acting in the Underground: Life as a Hare Krishna Devotee in the Soviet Republic of Lithuania (1979–1989)." *Religion and Society in Central and Eastern Europe* 7(1), 9–21.

Radhadesh. (2022). "Radhadesh." Facebook page. www.facebook.com/Radhadesh.

Radhadesh. (no date). "Radhadesh Chateau de Petite Somme." Website. https://radhadesh.com/.

Robison, C. (2016). "Daiva Varṇāśrama Dharma and the Formation of Modern Vaiṣṇava Subjects in the International Society for Krishna Consciousness, Mumbai." *Nidan: International Journal for Indian Studies* 1(2). https://journals.co.za/doi/abs/10.10520/EJC200060.

Rochford, E. B., Jr. (1982). "Recruitment Strategies, Ideology, and Organization in the Hare Krishna Movement." *Social Problems* 29, 399–410.

Rochford, E. B., Jr. (1985). *Hare Krishna in America.* New Brunswick, NJ: Rutgers University Press.

Rochford, E. B., Jr. (1988). "Movement and Public in Conflict: Values, Finances and the Decline of Hare Krishna." In J. T. Richardson, ed., *Money and Power in the New Religions*. Lewiston, NY: E. Mellen Press, pp. 271–303.

Rochford, E. B., Jr. (1989). "Factionalism, Group Defection, and Schism in the Hare Krishna Movement." *Journal for the Scientific Study of Religion* 28, 162–79.

Rochford, E. B., Jr. (1998). "Reactions of Hare Krishna Devotees to Scandals of Leaders' Misconduct." In A. D. Shupe, ed., *Wolves within the Fold: Religious Leadership and Abuses of Power*. New Brunswick, NJ: Rutgers University Press, pp. 101–17.

Rochford, E. B., Jr. (1999). "Prabhupada Centennial Survey: A Summary of the Final Report." *ISKCON Communications Journal* 7(1). https://content.isk con.org/icj/7_1/71rochford.html.

Rochford, E. B., Jr. (2007a). *Hare Krishna Transformed*. New York, NY: New York University Press.

Rochford, E. B., Jr. (2007b). "Social Building Blocks of New Religious Movements: Organization and Leadership." In D. G. Bromley and S. Henking, eds., *Teaching New Religious Movements*. New York, NY: Oxford University Press, pp. 159–85.

Rochford, E. B., Jr. (2009). "Succession, Religious Switching, and Schism in the Hare Krishna Movement." In J. R. Lewis and S. M. Lewis, eds., *Sacred Schisms: How Religions Divide*. New York, NY: Cambridge University Press, pp. 265–86.

Rochford, E. B., Jr. (2016). "The Changing Faces of God: The Hinduization of the Hare Krishna Movement." In E. Barker, ed., *Revisionism and Diversification in New Religious Movements*. London: Routledge, pp. 31–46.

Rochford, E. B., Jr. (2018). "Aligning Hare Krishna: Political Activists, Hippies, and Hindus." *Nova Religio* 22(1), 34–58. https://doi.org/10.1525/nr.2018.22.1.34.

Rochford, E. B., Jr. (2020). "Boundary and Identity Work among Hare Krishna Children." In S. B. Ridgely, ed., *The Study of Children in Religions: A Methods Handbook*. New York: New York University Press, pp. 95–107. https://doi.org/10.18574/9780814777466-009.

Rochford, E. B., Jr. and Heinlein, J. (1998). "Child Abuse in the Hare Krishna Movement: 1971–1986." *ISKCON Communications Journal* 6(1). https://content.iskcon.org/icj/6_1/6_1rochford.html.

Roof, W. C. (2001). *Spiritual Marketplace: Baby Boomers and the Remaking of American Religion*. Princeton, NJ: Princeton University Press.

Rose, K. S. (2020). "Lotuses in Muddy Water: Fracked Gas and the Hare Krishnas at New Vrindaban, West Virginia." *American Quarterly* 72(3), 749–69. https://doi.org/10.1353/aq.2020.0043.

Rosen, S. (2006). *Essential Hinduism.* Westport, CT: Praeger.

Shani, G. (2021). "Towards a Hindu Rashtra: Hindutva, Religion, and Nationalism in India." *Religion, State and Society* 49(3), 264–80. https://doi.org/10.1080/09637494.2021.1947731.

Sharma, S. (2014). Requesting Travel Restrictions Placed on HH Hridayananda Das Goswami to Be Lifted. *Change.org.* www.change.org/p/iskcon-gbc-requesting-travel-restrictions-placed-on-hh-hridayananda-das-goswami-to-be-lifted.

Sheludko, M. (2022). "Russo-Ukrainian War and Problems of Violence Justification among Russian and Ukrainian Vaishnavas." Paper presented at The Intersection of Hinduism and Contemporary Society conference, Oxford Centre for Hindu Studies, June 2–3. https://ochs.org.uk/wp-content/uploads/2022/05/Intersection-without-banner-art.pdf.

Shinn, L. D. (1987). *The Dark Lord: Cult Images and the Hare Krishnas in America.* Philadelphia, PA: Westminster Press.

Sinha, V. (2019). "Modern Hindu Diaspora(s)." In T. Brekke, ed., *The Oxford History of Hinduism: Modern Hinduism.* Oxford: Oxford University Press, pp. 179–99. https://doi.org/10.1093/oso/9780198790839.003.0011.

Smullen, M. (2019). "New North Carolina School 'Goloka' Sees Rapid Growth." *ISKCON News*, October 14. https://iskconnews.org/new-north-carolina-school-goloka-sees-rapid-growth,7124/.

Smullen, M. (2020). "Virtual Bhakti Retreat for Spanish Speakers Celebrates Tenth Installment." *ISKCON News*, August 28. https://iskconnews.org/virtual-bhakti-retreat-for-spanish-speakers-celebrates-tenth-installment,7477/.

Smullen, M. (2021a). "ISKCON Communications Journal Returns to Cover Important Issues After 15-Year Hiatus." *ISKCON News*, February 27. https://iskconnews.org/iskcon-communications-journal-returns-to-cover-important-issues-after-15-year-hiatus/.

Smullen, M. (2021b). "ISKCON Toronto to Hold Ratha-Yatra Drive-Thru Darshan." *ISKCON News*, July 17. https://iskconnews.org/iskcon-toronto-to-hold-ratha-yatra-drive-thru-darshan,7915/.

Snow, D. A., Ekland-Olson, S., and Zurcher, L. A. (1980). "Social Networks and Social Movements: A Microstructural Approach to Differential Recruitment." *American Sociological Review* 45(5), 787–801. https://doi.org/10.2307/2094895.

Snow, D. A., Rochford, E. B. Jr., Worden, S. K., and Benford, R. D. (1986). "Frame Alignment Processes, Micromobilization, and Movement Participation." *American Sociological Review* 51(5), 464–81.

Squarcini, F. (2000). "In Search of Identity within the Hare Krishna Movement: Memory, Oblivion and Thought Style." *Social Compass* 47(2), 253–71. https://doi.org/10.1177/003776800047002008.

Sri Mayapur Chandrodaya Mandir Temple of the Vedic Planetarium. (2013). "Founder's Vision." https://tovp.org/the-vision/.

Stark, R. (1996). "Why Religious Movements Succeed or Fail: A Revised General Model." *Journal of Contemporary Religion* 11(2), 133–46.

Stark, R. and Finke, R. (2000). *Acts of Faith: Explaining the Human Side of Religion*. Berkeley: University of California Press.

Tilly, C. (1978). *From Mobilization to Revolution*. Reading, MA: Addison-Wesley.

United Nations. (no date). "LGBTQI+." www.un.org/en/fight-racism/vulner able-groups/lgbtqi-plus.

US Court of Appeals for the Fourth Circuit. (1993). *United States of America, Plaintiff-appellee, v. Keith Gordon Ham, Justia*. https://law.justia.com/cases/ federal/appellate-courts/F2/998/1247/48079/.

Vaishnavas CARE. (2020). "Our Mission." Website. www.vaisnavascare.org/ our-mission.

Vaishnavi Ministry. (2021). "About Vaishnavi Ministry." Website. https://vaish naviministry.org/about-vaishnavi-ministry/.

Vande Berg, T. and Kniss, F. (2008). "ISKCON and Immigrants: The Rise, Decline, and Rise Again of a New Religious Movement." *Sociological Quarterly* 49(1), 79–104. https://doi.org/10.1111/j.1533-8525.2007.00107.x.

VIHE. (2019). "About VIHE." Website. https://vihe.org/retreats/aboutvihe .html.

VIHE. (2023). "Govardhana Retreat and Holy Name Retreat." Website. https:// vihe.org/retreats/.

Wilhelm, A. (2014). "Srila Prabhupada and the Gays, GALVA-108." www .galva108.org/single-post/2014/05/07/srila-prabhupada-and-the-gays.

Witzel, M. (2003). "Vedas and Upanisads." In G. Flood, ed., *The Blackwell Companion to Hinduism*. Oxford: Blackwell, pp. 68–98.

Zack, A. (2002). "A Dispute Resolution Programme for ISKCON." *ISKCON Communications Journal* 10. https://content.iskcon.org/icj/10/01-zack.html.

Zaidman, N. (2000). "The Integration of Indian Immigrants to Temples Run by North Americans." *Social Compass* 47(2), 205–19. https://doi.org/10.1177/ 003776800047002005.

Zald, M. N. and McCarthy, J. D., eds. (2017). *Social Movements in an Organizational Society: Collected Essays*. 1st ed. London: Routledge.

Zeller, B. E. (2021). "New Religious Movement Responses to COVID: Frame Alignment Strategies and Social Context." *Approaching Religion* 11(2), 62–81. https://doi.org/10.30664/ar.107731.

Acknowledgments

My sincere thanks go to a number of people who helped bring this Element to fruition. Firstly to E. Burke Rochford for originally inviting me to write it, and for his years of dedicated scholarship that have inspired much of the work that is at the heart of this Element. The Founding Editor of this Elements series, James R. Lewis, provided me with the opportunity to complete it, and the Series Editor Rebecca Moore had an endless supply of patience and support. The staff at Cambridge University Press have been exceptionally helpful throughout the publication process. My mother, Elizabeth Burt, introduced me to books and libraries, supported me in all my educational pursuits, and taught me how to think. My late sister, Miriam Burt, whose gracious parting gift has enabled me to pursue my academic goals, has helped me enormously even in her absence. Finally, thanks go to the members of the Hare Krishna movement whose persistence in pursuing their ideals has given me a great deal to write about. I owe a debt of gratitude to all.

Cambridge Elements ☰

New Religious Movements

Founding Editor

†James R. Lewis

Wuhan University

The late James R. Lewis was Professor of Philosophy at Wuhan University, China. He served as the editor or co-editor for four book series, was the general editor for the *Alternative Spirituality and Religion Review*, and the associate editor for the *Journal of Religion and Violence*. His publications include *The Cambridge Companion to Religion and Terrorism* (Cambridge University Press 2017) and *Falun Gong: Spiritual Warfare and Martyrdom* (Cambridge University Press 2018).

Series Editor

Rebecca Moore

San Diego State University

Rebecca Moore is Emerita Professor of Religious Studies at San Diego State University. She has written and edited numerous books and articles on Peoples Temple and the Jonestown tragedy. She has served as co-general editor or reviews editor of *Nova Religio* since 2000. Publications include *Beyond Brainwashing: Perspectives on Cult Violence* (Cambridge University Press 2018) and *Peoples Temple and Jonestown in the Twenty-First Century* (Cambridge University Press 2022).

About the Series

Elements in New Religious Movements go beyond cult stereotypes and popular prejudices to present new religions and their adherents in a scholarly and engaging manner. Case studies of individual groups, such as Transcendental Meditation and Scientology, provide in-depth consideration of some of the most well known, and controversial, groups. Thematic examinations of women, children, science, technology, and other topics focus on specific issues unique to these groups. Historical analyses locate new religions in specific religious, social, political, and cultural contexts. These examinations demonstrate why some groups exist in tension with the wider society and why others live peaceably in the mainstream. The series highlights the differences, as well as the similarities, within this great variety of religious expressions. To discuss contributing to this series please contact Professor Moore, remoore@sdsu.edu.

Cambridge Elements ≡

New Religious Movements

Elements in the Series

Printed in the United States
by Baker & Taylor Publisher Services